AF454148

WAR FOR THE DESTRUCTION OF INTELLIGENCE

Author: Joseph-Christos Kondylakis

Nuclear physicist with specialization in Nuclear Fission; former Assistant Technical Supervisor at the General Division of Nuclear Power Production in "Ontario Hydro" (Canada); former Systems Design and Development Manager in a Canadian company.

Publish on Demand, Inc.
© Fylatos Publishing,
Thessaloniki & Delaware 2019
Author: Joseph-Christos Kondylakis
Editor: Konstantinos Fylatos

© Fylatos Publishing
e-mail: contact@fylatos.com
web: www.fylatos.com

Pagination-Design: © Fylatos Publishing
ISBN: 978-618-5318-77-2

Joseph-Christos Kondylakis

WAR FOR THE DESTRUCTION OF INTELLIGENCE

Fylatos Publishing
Thessaloniki & Delaware
2019

Short Curriculum Vitae
of the author of this book:

Mr. Joseph-Christos Kondylakis was born in the city of Heraklion, Crete, Greece. He graduated with an 'Excellent' Degree from the Physics Department at *The Aristotle University of Thessaloniki (Greece)*. He has completed postgraduate studies in Nuclear Physics (M.Sc.) with specialization in Nuclear Fission (Applied and Theoretically) at *McGill University* (Canada), where he studied under a full Canadian scholarship. He has worked as Manager of Systems Design and Development in a prestigious Canadian company; also as an Assistant Technical Supervisor in the Headquarters of the General Division for the Production of Nuclear Fission Power in "Ontario Hydro" (Canada), and in *The Hellenic Centre for Marine Research (Greece)*. He has held many other important posts.

His scientific interests span multiple areas of research. He is actively involved in original Pure Scientific Research in many fields, such as (to name only a few) Physics, Mathematics, Information Technology, Electronics (SV1GZ), Medicine (oncology, psychology/psychiatry), Law, Philosophy, Ecology, International Relations, Orthodox Christianity, and many other fields. He has published fundamental and original articles in both Greek and International scientific journals. He is also a prolific author who has written numerous scientific articles which he has addressed to Embassies as well as to National & International Organizations.

Note:

The title of the original Greek book is as follows: "ΠΟΛΕΜΟΣ ΓΙΑ ΤΗΝ ΚΑΤΑΣΤΡΟΦΗ ΤΗΣ ΝΟΗΜΟΣΥΝΗΣ" authored by Ιωσήφ-Χρήστος Κ. Κονδυλάκης.

Note: This book in English language contains much additional information to the original Greek book.

Author' correspondence: Mr. Joseph-Christos Kondylakis,
Anavissos' Greater Area,
Postal Code: 19013,Attiki, GREECE
E-mail: sifiskon@otenet.gr

Acknowledgments:

The author wishes to express his deep gratitude & thanks to the translator of his book, Dr Tina Lekka, for her excellent intellectual efforts and her grasp of the topic, which have ensured the quality of scientific precision and the understanding in the English language of my book, originally written in the Greek language. All errors and omissions remain my own.

I also want to to thank the reviewer of my publishing house "Fylatos" for (his or her) very useful comments, and of course I want much to thank my Publisher "Fylatos" for our very good and pleasant cooperation, in publishing my book (in English ard in Greek languages).

I devote this book to my Lovely Family...

MAIN TABLE OF CONTENTS

WAR FOR THE DESTRUCTION OF INTELLIGENCE

By Josef-Christos Kondylakis, 2001.

Nuclear Physicist/Information Technology Specialist. Formerly an Assistant Technical Supervisor in Nuclear Fission Reactors 'Plants Headquarters. Formerly a Manager in Systems Designing and Development (Canada). Currently working for *the Hellenic Centre for Marine Research, in Greece.*

In Lieu of an Introduction

This book is an introduction to the topic of the *War for the Destruction of Intelligence* (IDW), as it is being conducted against Nations, Organizations and individuals (for instance, against State Organizations, the Armed Forces as well as against the Educational and Research system, Commercial organizations and extremely knowledgeable humans and citizens endowed with high intelligence and so on and so forth). This book is also an exposition of particular methods for masterminding IDW whilst suggestions for further scientific research on this topic are also offered. The critical significant of the Protection of human cognitive Intelligence is because of the fact that:

ALL !! PURPOSEFUL HUMAN DECISIONS DEPEND ONLY ON TWO FACTORS:

(1) THE AVAILABLE INFORMATION TO THE HUMAN, AND

(2) THE GOGNITIVE INTELLIGENCE OF THE HUMAN...

Abstract

The present article serves as an introduction to the topic of Intelligence Destruction War (henceforth IDW), as the latter is being waged against Nations, Organizations and individuals (e.g. against State Institutions, the Armed Forces including the Educational and Research System, Commercial organizations as well as against erudite individuals of high intelligence, civilians and the like). Some of the methods employed for the said War are described and suggestions are made for further research on the topic. That said, it should be noted that the present article is a scientific study and treats the aforementioned topic as a **Nationally unifying one** (after all, some fine ideas may originate from all political parties, provided that one remains open-minded) and under no circumstances should it be regarded as a study which can cause divisive politics. It is, therefore, hoped that the present paper will stimulate both critical and novel thinking and that it will serve as a systematic study that is germane to the topic of IDW.

Keywords: **Intelligence; War; Defense; Attack; Research**

Note to the Reader:

The present scientific study is a continuation of article [1]. Both studies aspire to function as background to legal protection against IDW. Furthermore, the author of this study maintains that Nations and States must be respectful of Human Rights as these have been laid out in the legal texts of International Organizations such as the United Nations, the Council of Europe, the European Union etc. It must be clearly stated here that 'good' and 'bad' individuals, in the sense of their adherence to Justice and Morality, exist in every Nation and State. This study is dedicated to all fights for Human Rights in the hope that a more Righteous future will prevail for the sake of Humanity [32], [35].

PS: Article [1] entitled 'Constructive intelligence as a lawful good' by Josef-Christos Kondylakis, published in the Greek law magazine *Criminal Justice* (October 1999, pages 1055-1056), is included in the present study in the form of a supplement.

Contents of this section

1. Definitions of Terms

Intelligence of the Human Being [1] refers to the capability for problem-solving (scientific, military problems and the like) and/or to the non-random choice of an optimum solution pertaining to a decision-making problem, by means of an algorithm, which might include a series of logical processes (such as the N iterative cycles question(s) process: *Why, Because, Does It Have the Sense of*?), on the causes that are to be understood [2], [3], where N is a possitive integer number.

Intelligence of the Human Organization [1] refers to the effectiveness of solutions to problems involving Organizations (e.g. the State, the Armed Forces, Commerce organizations); in particular, the term refers to decision−making that is optimum- solution oriented both time-wise and space-wise and varying according to each case [1]. The said term also refers to the optimum implementation of the previously mentioned decisions.

Optimum Decision [1] refers to the type of decision that maximizes the possibility for the realization of a series of targets, both spatially and temporally, yet simultaneously safeguarding that any restrictions set in relation to the set of targets will be obeyed.

Intelligence Destruction War (IDW) [1] refers to the destruction of Human Intelligence and/or of the Intelligence of the Human Organization; the destruction in question might be owing either to malicious or criminal negligence be it partial or total, a temporary or a permanent one (the aforementioned War might take place in the level of natural persons, legal entities, Nation and State). In its gravest form, the author of the present study thinks that the said War can culminate into treason offences against the Nation and into High Treason [4].

Note: An example of logical cognitive Intelligence Reasoning syllogism is :

[Assumptions and Restrictions made...],Because,because...because, for these Reasons,

My opinion is...

(s.n. In emotional Reasoning the Reason(s) may be of emotional type. Also, it may exist Mixed Logical & emotional cognitive Intelligence syllogism(s)).

2. Introduction

In our sensory world, everything is dependent upon natural laws, 'chance' as well as upon human and animal decisions [1].

The conclusion to be drawn from the aforementioned parameters is that human's intentional impact on either an earthly or an unearthly environment is associated with both decision-making and the implementation of those decisions [1]. Consequently, the choice of a set of targets that it is appropriate for the temporal-spatial needs coupled with the optimum implementation of this set of targets, is directly correlated both with human intelligence and human organizations' intelligence [1].

Given all of the above, it can be concluded that due to the ramifications brought about by 'idiotic' decisions, the destruction of human intelligence and human organizations' intelligence can potentially result in the destruction of humans and of human organizations alike. Furthermore, it is also possible that both the individual and/or a human organization with an even partially destroyed intelligence are at risk of becoming, at times even unperceived to them, docile victims executing the orders of people and/or the organization that conduct IDW against them.

The above-mentioned points demonstrate that one cannot overstate the need for realization and then the profound understanding of the fact that IDW does take place against people and / or organizations; similarly, it is equally crucial that defense mechanisms be developed to combat IDW on the human, the Nation and the European Union levels.

Note to the reader/researcher:

As certain methods of IDW are classifiable under many categories, textual repetitions are bound to occur in different sections of the present study, nevertheless, in this way, enriching the coherency of the book.

3. An overview of a number of IDW Methods

The overall rationale underpinning the IDW methods is to either obstruct or diminish the efficacy of problem-solving processes, pertaining to Person and / or to the Human Organization.

3.1. Lack of Motivation and Lack of Rewarding of Motivation

When organizations fall short in motivation (i.e. when there is no financial differentiation in terms of salaries and bonuses, no advancement opportunities in the career ladder alongside with the inability of companies to promote the right employees in the right posts and to foster an active interest in employment, when there are no morale-boosting awards and the like), then, in that case, there is no interest in the cultivation of intelligence either and what arises is a tendency for indifference and idleness.

Conversely, bonuses (be they monetary or moral) that are being distributed according to the principles of meritocracy alongside the meritocratic assessment and pay of advisors and instructors as well as of the scientifically trained, specialized personnel) are measurements that may attract and stimulate the interest of potentially highly intelligent and equally highly qualified human workforce [14], [25].

Of particular mention and certainly worth-delving into are the cases where not only are incentives for the enhancement of intelligence non-existent, but, worse even, anti-incentives obliterating intelligence abound --- by way of illustration, let us consider a state where the jobs that enjoy high payment are the ones that serve to further hypnotize the public's intellectual faculties (one may refer here to the singer's profession – especially those ones whose repertoire includes a single verse which is incessantly repeated and in such a pitch, at that, that ultimately ends up being painful to the ear, thus rendering any either logical or emotional conversation impossible) are of particular mention and certainly worth-delving into. Another example germane to the discussion is the footballer's profession, that through its monotonous perpetuation, extremely often shown by the Media, usually (and possibly deliberately so as part of the IDW) takes center stage, thus causing delays in the broadcasting of news (the latter may even include information on European Union state leaders' summits). Added to this is the exorbitant daily pay of second-grade educational level manual laborers, whilst at the same time professionals in high intelligence posts watch their incomes plunging. And it is precisely those individuals (e.g. stellar scientists holding postgraduate degrees as well as other working people engaged in intellectual and creative activities) who have the potential to raise the public's intelligence level. This whole situation makes it practically unfeasible for fine scientists to purchase the extremely costly academic textbooks required for their research purposes; in turn, this results in the impoverishment of their quality of life as well as in the degradation of their standard of living. Furthermore, because of the financial hardship, this very same category of people is deprived of any opportunity for social recognition and, as a consequence, their intelligence and drive for maverick research suffers a blow, while their work performance drops especially when compared to their actual abilities. The long term, short term, and medium-term ramifications may turn out to be disastrous for the nation's own interests, not least because the Nation's abilities for development and/or the effectiveness of scientific analysis and the optimization of national problem-solving efficacy are seriously compromised – in turn, this might lead to the increased possibility for a plethora of catastrophic future consequences, alongside with lost opportunities national interests-wise.

In our view, the augmenting of 'idiocy-promoting' income sources that operate in parallel with the diminishing of income deriving from 'intelligence sources and creative knowledge' is, in essence, the most effective method used in a war aiming at both intelligence's and culture's destruction as well as an organization's (i.e. Nation) destruction.

This scenario gets even bleaker when people are taught by the Mass Media to use the 'products' and the 'services' originating from sources of IDIOCY whilst remaining in the dark on scientific, technological and culture-enriching developments (with the possible exception of medical advancements).

3.2. Deficiencies or Destruction of the Harmonious Hierarchy of Organizations (e.g. Nepotism, Corruption, etc.)

Organizations' creative hierarchy is instrumental in determining the decisions that need to be executed as well as in fostering a climate that encourages both the organization's work performance and resources' availability optimization.

Regrettably, the reality is that there are vitally devastating situations threatening human organizations (such as the State, Private companies and the like). For instance, in the Public Services and in the Armed Forces there might be certain employee groups, such as brilliant scientists and university professors, as well as individuals who either excel at the execution of military exercises, or are highly distinguished in real-time situations. And yet, all these aforementioned groups are poorly paid and overlooked. Worse even, these employees do not get promoted in the appropriate ranks, while job positions are offered instead to individuals who have been favored because they have been pulling strings (i.e. eclectic relationships or political alliances, fraudulent practices, oblique intervention from foreign nations and interests and so on and so forth). As a result of all the above, both the human organization's (i.e. State, Armed Forces) intelligence and the individual's intelligence (due to psychosomatic conditions induced by feelings of unfair treatment) are crashed.

Perhaps a classic case-study of IDW in the Armed Forces is the obliteration of the brightest officers right from the outset of their careers by means of reducing them to nothing more than a statistic of plain soldiers or sergeants, even though they are Professors at University or Excellent Scientists. One reason for this tactic lies in the enforcement of relevant regulations that apply in the armed forces, though the former may have come into effect through the implicit influence of alien forces which have exploited the psychological complexes often attributed to people serving in the military (i.e. egotism and the like). Be that as it may, the ramifications of such a practice not only are deeply damaging for the Nation but they also have a profoundly harmful effect on the Nation's interests that may even extend to territorial jeopardy (for instance, as a potential result of either unwise decisions or of the failure to resolve any problems in the best possible way, by considering not only the spatial and temporal parameters, but also by judging on the optimum solution that it is befitting to the situation at hand in times of crisis[5]).

In addition, it needs to be stressed here that nowadays, in this era of cutting-edge-technology, of the specialization of knowledge, and also of the globally perceived interdisciplinary knowledge certain people may be deemed irreplaceable. By the same token, should a State or a private business fail to use the services of these people, the former may face dreadful consequences – in the sense that they may not succeed in making the correct decisions and, in extension, serious damage may be inflicted upon the State in both the internal plane and in its foreign policy plane. Likewise, a private business may be forced to bankruptcy.

3.3. Deficiencies or Destruction of the Quality of knowledge (Education, Information Outlets and the like)

Certain IDW tactics include the use of sensational jargon from the domain of psychological manipulation in conjunction with the ruination of linguistic accuracy in the dissemination of information; also, the accounts and the highlighting of trivial chunks of information; the distraction of the public's attention by means of spreading a **plethora of irrelevant information** while, at the same time, the principal and key information remains concealed; the emphasis on partial information along with the blurring of the 'whole picture' of the matter at hand; one-sided information and the simultaneous silencing of multiple views on a topic (perhaps the sole source of information in this particular case are a few NATO manuals and scientific journals in Nations' war industries). In addition, the overabundance of **instruction manuals** (especially on the use of computers) whilst there is either a scarcity of manuals and books on the **understanding of basic principles** and on the details involving **the designing /manufacturing of new products** or the considerable lack of authoritative **academic textbooks** with the simultaneous distribution of **highly-advertised, yet very poor ones**.

Furthermore, the excessive and in a widespread scale advertising through the Media of Mass Communication {Television, the Press, Radio and the like} of topics that utterly stupefy the audience and shatter its intelligence (for example via the moronic astrological 'advice' or the televised quizzes that serve in the memorization of useless information and so on and so forth) constitute IDW against the State's citizenry. As this were not enough, the aforementioned practices work in parallel with an attempt to completely suppress any available sources of intelligent information such as scientific, technological achievements, as well as any philosophical advances and any progress that may have been made in both scientific and constructive societal discourse.

Listed among the methods of IDW is also teaching from textbooks characterized either by low quality or by information that is likely to be misleading. In addition, there might be teachers who are implicitly (and many times involuntarily so) influenced either by foreign states' interests or by foreign advisors working in National organizations, which promote foreign interests, thereby influencing the **direction** of decision-making (be those decisions either State or Science- related) .

Ultimately, they might leave to the citizens and National organizations merely the freedom to form the trivial details.

During the course of scientific/technological progress it is perhaps feasible for monetary interests to allow for the widespread advertising and promotion of fundamental theories and ideas towards to specific knowledge directions – the latter might be originating from **excessively advertised scientific institutions.** This leaves the freedom of the arranging of detail(s) to others, and probably also with a certain degree of control exercised upon both global scientific journals and upon the way ideas are promoted in the global network of computers, aka the INTERNET, perhaps, again, by means of controlling the most popular search engines, etc.

The lack of funding for the setting up of libraries along with the injudicious choice of textbooks in scientific libraries is yet another effective method of IDW. Not least because of the fact that it deprives one of **information which is of high quality** and, in this respect, the cornerstone of optimum decision-making.

One-sided information narrows our intellectual horizons. So, let us keep in mind that a fine idea may originate either from any political party or any thinkable individual (even from a child or someone who is incognizant of our science). Equally, a fine idea may lead to a very effective solution to a problem, hence it is important that we listen about it attentively – needless to say we must also be courteous enough to both acknowledge and reward the source of the fine idea, so that the individual may be encouraged to continue offering us their ideas.

Let us now turn to another example of IDW. More specifically, I wish to discuss the academic examinations, such as the final exams in Greece, for entering tertiary education. It is often the case, that the exam topics are extremely easy; then, the majority of candidates answer to the exam questions correctly; consequently, successful candidates' selection is based on criteria that are irrelevant to the essence of the exam questions. Such criteria may include calligraphy, a well-presented written text as well as spelling and neatness in writing, i.e. a deletions and smudges-free text . It is really problematic for an examiner to correct the said examination paper with a view to create the differentiation between a high grade, say 19/20 and a failed one, say 18,5/20. Conversely, choosing the successful candidates through very challenging topics is bound to by far distinguish the candidate who made it through the task from the one who has failed to do so. As a result, the winning candidates will have demonstrated their skillfulness in substantial criteria: critical thinking abilities, ample knowledge, ability to resolve difficult problems and the like. One should be reminded here that geniuses in the field of Sciences were notorious for their poor handwriting and were deemed as sloppy writers, an 'accusation' which makes it sensible to assume that, should they ever sat in exams where the topics given were too easy, those geniuses would probably be deemed as 'unsuccessful candidates', as there would be other candidates more dexterous at the aforementioned irrelevant and trivial selection criteria.

It goes without saying that future scientists, of high creative intelligence and knowledge, are the foundations of the Nation's future well-being since, thanks to the former, the human factor approach involving the optimum decision-making process (not only temporally and spatially-wise but also in accordance with for each particular case) is enhanced.

3.4. Damaging Mass Media Productions

Normally, the Mass Media serves the information and entertainment of the public. However, qualitative criteria should be implemented for both functions, because Justice as well as the intelligence and the psychosomatic health of human beings must be safeguarded. Likewise, the quality of entertainment provided should preponderate in terms of human civilization when compared to the propagation of animalistic behaviors and instincts. As far as the information offered by the Media is concerned, the practice of omitting the broadcasting of important and meaningful news on the fields of science and human sciences is deemed as IDW. By contrast, what the media engages in is the propagation of lengthy, tedious details which more often than not hide the essence of the news, thereby making the audience watch 'The news' for extended periods of time without them realizing what has actually happened. At the same time, they are turned into mere receivers of emotional influence as these are exemplified in the form of dramatics. This aforementioned practice leads to the weakening of the viewer's listener's and reader's critical thinking and intelligence faculties.

Statistically speaking, Mass Media news pertains almost exclusively to the presentation of disturbing or tragic events, whilst the presentation of positive or agreeable news or the type of news related scientific progress announcements is practically non-existent (with the exception of medical news). In this respect, the public's perception of societal reality is significantly distorted, thus cultivating a climate of indifference, a tolerance for grave crimes and also a feeling of hostility towards the 'Other' human being. In other words, not only does the individual become socially isolated, but also more social problems emerge, which dramatically undermine the efficacy of the use of intelligence. By contrast, the latter is steeply augmented within a creative social environment as this is exemplified in the context of a creative family, Justice and creative ethics (e.g. the doctrines of the Christian Faith).

We are now moving on to another IDW method employed by the Mass Media, namely the plethora of productions and advertisements, which feature astrologers, sorcerers and other similar types of 'charlatans-fraudsters'. This category of people stupefies the audience by means of taking advantage of their vital emotional issues (this usually adheres more to the female viewers). Sadly, however, similarly idiotic methods have been used with a view to stupefy even ... aircraft pilots (see, for instance, the so-called 'biorhythms' technique). Needless to say, the IDW method, that relies heavily on superstition, has damaging effects not least because individuals end up attracting misfortunes for the simple reason that they seek out for them when, in actuality, they connect IRRELEVANT facts of their lives with those which their very superstitions have forced them to except to happen to them.

In addition, another IDW tactic includes television quizzes with an excessive emphasis on memorization of useless knowledge which thus exclude the application of critical thinking and intelligence, by rewarding useless knowledge instead.

Another consequence of the terrorism propagated by the Mass Media is that they intimidate the citizen, thus rending them more susceptible to the mind control, that statistically imposed to human thought by the Mass Media. Examples of this type of control over the human thinking include, among other things, what the conversation topics should be (agenda setting) and which of them should be of interest to the public. Yet, control is also expanded in the sphere of the public's behavior (including implicit and/or explicit influences from peers who watch mass media productions as advertisements and soap-operas/Classical Conditioning- Ivan Pavlov) as to the latter's actions and rewards/Operant Conditioning-Skinner). Overall, statistically speaking, the public's attitude resembles a 'robot' that is 'remotely-guided' or *"telecontrolled"* by the Mass Media. Statistically speaking, too, through this specific method the public's intelligence and creative ambitions are likely to suffer a substantial decline. This decline is, in the long run, equally detrimental to national interests, as there is bound to be a widespread reduction in the number of people who are highly intelligent and who have the know-how for making the optimum decisions, in the face of highly complex and sophisticated problems that potentially arise from the extremely rapid – or perhaps uncontrollable, in some of its aspects – progress in the fields of science, technology and international relations.

Furthermore, the customary refusal to inform the public on breakthrough scientific discoveries (with the exception of medical science) relinquishes any chances of fostering an intellectual and intelligent public sphere. This is owed to the fact that the body of citizens is deprived of the possibility to develop interests and to encourage a discourse that will be focusing on scientific matters and that will be informed by sensible problematization on the topics under discussion. As a consequence, the public's intelligence and quality of knowledge level drops dramatically. The mass media, on the other hand, have created role models that supposedly reflect the youth's 'dreams'. These role models, however, aim at mimicking footballers, singers who enjoy success with the lowest of quality songs and, last but not least, actors of loose morals. As a consequence of this mass media tactic, young people are discouraged from looking up to eminent scientists, as well as to individuals, excelling at creative intelligence and intelligentsia and to creative culture personalities.

The productions encouraged by the Mass Media have the potential to manipulate the public's perception [26], in the sense that the Mass Media are adept at perception management through their enforcing to the public of possible interpretations (of the spectacle) that are in accordance with the interests of the media producers. By way of illustration, let us consider the American films with the abundant representation of violence and terrorism, which are said to statistically increase the possibility for people to perceive either a certain behavior and/or an event as life-threatening ones. Assuming that a man lives in a constantly threatening environment (the latter may as well be the result of the violence and terrorism perpetuated by the Media), then his considerable creative ability is negatively affected too. Simply put, this person is afflicted with IDW, thereby the efficacy of his reasoning abilities is seriously impaired. It then emerges that the impact of IDW on the public's perception functions may prove disastrous for human intelligence, because it might lead to erroneous interpretation of facts/events and the same might apply for problem-solving processes. Should the latter occur, then both incorrect and misleading 'solutions' are bound to be given to problems involving 'reality' as this is conceptualized by the human agent, and it is precisely on the grounds of this subjective reality that all decisions be made. All things considered, this is yet another IDW tactic.

In our time, another global IDW method involves the control exerted over the global computers' INTERNET network through the most popular **search engines** (research programs) such as *Yahoo, Alta-Vista, Lycos, Netscape, Microsoft, Google* and the like. Once you enter 'keywords' in these search engines, they provide you with address of a World Wide Web page, where one can find information relating to the 'keywords' given. Now, it appears that the highly popular search engines (all of them in USA) collaborate in order to control the information extracted from the INTERNET. Consider, for instance, the following true incident:

The author of the present study is the mastermind behind the theory called 'A theory on the evolution of an intelligent ecosystem', which significantly modifies the Darwinian theory of evolution in the context of an ecosystem and thus to render Darwin's theory even more relevant to our era of high intelligence/knowledge and technology. The theory in question was published in the scientific journal of the Associations of Dutch and French Theoretical Biologists 'Anta Biotheoretica', 45 (2), June 1997, p. 181-182 and in the author's web address which was the following: www.ncmr.gr/Kondylakis.html.

Very malicious interests stopped latter the operation of this author's Internet site and also stopped, twice, for years, the operation of his professional email communications in his work (HCMR, Greece). They blocked his telephone and fax communications with the Aristotle University of Thessaloniki, Greece (from which he has graduated with "Excellent" degree), stopped his emails & fax communications with the Physics Dept. of McGill University, Canada (from which he has post-graduated with a Canadian Scholarship) & stopped his communications elsewhere. Also, with a huge violation of the European Treaty(-/ies) in the European Parliament, during last years, the Petition Committee of European Parliament do not register his Petitions to European Parliament, even when many of his Petitions are concern ng Vital Themes such as: the International Nuclear Safety & Security[39], Fundamental Theoretical Oncology scientific research[38], Control of Humanity, E.T.C. (and his relevant actions for help to European Ombudsman(s) and to European Union Court resulted in unfair results), and also illegally they block/stop this author (a Nuclear Physicist) communications with the main telephone and fax of the International "Atomic"(NUCLEAR!) Energy Agency (I.A.E.A.)E.T.C... [36].

The Theory on the development of an intelligent ecosystem bears important implications for the fields of Biology, Intelligence, Sociology as well as of Ethics, Religion, Philosophy and also of Economics, Psychology and broadly speaking for many scientific branches and technology. It is therefore a Theory of vital importance, that should become known to the global scientific community.

In addition, the author of the present study (who has also conducted scientific research in information technology) and who has attempted 2-4 times in a year-span (and this is also confirmable by the most experienced scientist in Information Technology in his work) to submit the address for the aforementioned study on ecosystems to the search engines *Yahoo, AltaVista, Lycos, Netscape, Microsoft* and to a few more others (a Greece-based one included). And yet, except from *AltaVista*, all other search engines declined to approve the presentation of his theory's web address, thus blocking the opportunities for a major scientific discovery to attract global attention.

As the consequences of the aforementioned incident may be ungraspable for some readers, it must be highlighted that the lack of a POPULAR search engine, that will be operating with the support of the European Union, will result in important scientific discoveries by European Scientists as well as discoveries of new and innovative commercial products failing to become globa ly known — and the cost of this omission is bound to be critical for the European scientific research, the economy and other critical ventures.

3.5. Workplace and Living Ecosystems that Cause Irreplaceable Damage to Creative Intelligence.

It is quite obvious that there are a number of factors that seriously undermine the efficacy of both the use of intelligence and of intellectual labor. These factors include living and/or working within ecosystems surrounded by vibrations caused by pneumatic drills, strong pollutants by exhaustion fumes, very strong traffic & street noise(s), lack of sufficient working space (i.e. inadequate furnishing and other essentials) as well as spaces with either poor lighting or depressing coloring. Equally problematic is the excessively bright and irritating coloring that induces not only visual but also emotional fatigue as well as the utter lack of trees and plants and, additionally, absence of creative decoration, poor ergonomics and equally poor sanitation conditions and critical transportation issues that affect arrival and departure from the workplace (or residential address). In other words, all the aforementioned conditions may be deemed as an additional effective IDW method.

If one wishes to analyze this further, he/she could argue that, when it comes to resolving highly complex problems rather than those involving manual labor, there is a significant qualitative difference between a working space in an old building at the ground floor of a very degraded area and a working space located either in a beautiful Greek island or, say, in a pine-covered habitat in a suitable, functionally-designed building [27]. In a similar vein, we have instances of IDW in cases of a person living in a sunless basement apartment (mostly because he/she is a scientist unable to afford a better residence) whose living conditions are in stark contrast to another person's own (e.g. a wealthy footballer star), especially when the latter resides near a quiet beautiful island beach.

3.6. Disastrous State Policies (bureaucracy, time-consuming procedures, special favors, favoritism, deficit in organization, etc.).

It is indisputable that bureaucracy exercises a kind of psychological war on the efficacy of the use of intelligence, because of a number of reasons: first of all, it is nerve-racking; secondly, it is an excessive loss of time on irrelevant and often pointless procedures; thirdly, it distracts one from their main job; last but not least, it is the source of dismay (especially in cases when problems are caused by employees who resort to extortion in order to receive briberies). Overall, bureaucracy is a powerful IDW technique.

Favoritism and lack of meritocracy (due to, e.g. friends or political connections), coupled with special favors, produces incompetent supervisors who, often motivated by fear of losing their own posts, are at pains — usually through authoritarian tactics — to relinquish both the intelligence and the passion for work of their subordinates (e.g. by means of forcing the latter to blindly obey their orders,often using the 'termination of employment' narrative or other psychological tactics) — orders which may in the long run be proved to be calamitous for both the Organization (Nation, commercial enterprise) and the public (e.g. in Nuclear Reactors Organizations [13],[39], Genetics, Information Technology and the like. In addition, the aforementioned supervisors tend to assign the blame for the own failures on their subordinates while, at the same time, they favor and help climb the corporate ladder those employees who are worse than them, performance-wise, in an effort to propagate their own poor leadership, and so on and so forth). As a ramification of all the above tactics that foster the War Against Intelligence, it is the emergence of counter-motives, which impede the use and cultivation of intelligence, thus bringing about the resignation of excellent employees from the organization they work for; in turn, this results in the destruction of Human organization intelligence. The resignation factor aside, such practices may also impel extremely capable employees to remain passive ones, solely waiting for the time of their retirement, with their intelligence wrecked and with a load of psychosomatic illnesses.

3.7. Income related legislation that is detrimental to creative intelligence

A secure tactic for the destruction of the intelligence of the most excellent and knowledgeable people of the Nation includes legislature, laws and court decisions that favor the maximization of profit of 'stupefying the masses sources' (e.g. football, businesses promoting low-taste songs, illiterate labor in the construction business{for example, contractors}etc.), while, at the same time, the monetary gain of 'intelligence sources' dwindles (consider, for example the specialized medical doctors working in the National Health System who receive a salary smaller than a sanitation worker; or scientists with postgraduate degrees that earn a salary that is lower than one of a sergeant). It all comes down, in other words, to a IDW because the living standards are seriously undermined, while giving rise to social injustice and to an appreciation for a social status that it is insulting to creative intelligence. In addition, it renders the sources of creative intelligence incapable of acquiring the necessary equipment for their work (e.g. very costly scientific textbooks and the like). By contrast, it distracts them from concentrating in their work since, due to financial hardship, the intelligence sources in question are compelled to engage in activities that are both incongruent with their research interests and also time-consuming (e.g. the inability to purchase a car results in considerable waste of time as the person has to use the means of public transport, and the same applies for the time-consuming domestic repairs). This whole situation, in conjunction with the inability (again due to financial difficulties) for resting the mind via quality entertainment is essentially the gravestone of the efficacy, creativity and innovative use of intelligence. It is a commonplace to use the example of internationally renowned University

Professors in the Former Soviet Union who sought employment as... construction workers (!) in Greece.

Furthermore, the more the income of the sources of idiotizing the public is augmented and consequently maximized, the more their own preferred culture and so-called 'civilization' dominates. So much so, in fact, that it tends to be regarded as 'National' Culture – needless to say, this happens because the said sources own the financial means to fund what they perceive as 'culture', whereas, at the same time, both the culture and the creative civilization of the 'intelligence sources' are annihilated, since the creatively intelligent people lack the financial resources to both sustain and develop their own creative culture. The consequences for the Nation are perilous: all Mass Media outlets promote the culture of sheer idiotizing and the creative intellectualism generated by the 'intelligence sources' has almost been erased by Mass Media productions. In addition, the psychological pressure exercised by the Media upon the audiences for the 'socially accepted' norm forces highly educated individuals to comply with the dominant culture of the stupefycation sources that take center stage financially-wise.

At the other end of the spectrum, it is known that the massive scientific and technological progress in, say, Canada and USA and in other economically developed European States is owed – to a large extent – to the very satisfactory salaries offered to the 'creative intelligence sources'; the latter, through their work and the application of smart and informed decisions contribute to the prosperity of the organization's they work for(be it the State, an Institution etc.) in the short-term, medium-term and long-term scale. Consequently, provided that the Government implements a Humanitarian policy it will become financially viable to welfare benefits to the State's citizens, as well as to special need People (an admirable example in this respect is the Netherlands' financial policy).

In order for the creatively intelligent and knowledgeable person to be productive, they need the right motivation and motivation bonuses in addition to the qualities and resources required, [14], a certain degree of financial comfort, a living and working ecosystem that allows for a decent and comfortable standard of living and leisure time. Additionally, they need a constructive social life (allow me here to also mention the need for constructive religion too – e.g. Christianity – that will provide the moral framework for support in hard and highly distressful times) as well as an irritation-free, trouble-free and illness-free environment; in addition, they need opportunities for creative entertainment that will be paired with agreeable and intelligent information by the Mass Media and the other sources of news dissemination.

3.8. Psychological war against individuals of high intelligence and knowledge and against people employed in key posts (e.g. scientists, diplomats, military officers, journalists and the like).

Certain States, whose actions reveal a hegemonic mindset, have been at pains to destroy the stellar scientists and highly-qualified individuals from other States who have the potential to make a significant contribution to the progress of their own State. This tactic enables the hegemonic State to safeguard both its hegemony on a global scale and its control over States. Furthermore, through either the destruction or the serious curtailing of the influential individuals who may evolve into competitors and a force to be reckoned with in the fields of Economics and/or Science, the hegemonic state enforces its hegemony on other States. Defense-wise, Nations and States should consider their highly-qualified citizens as foremost National Interest and National Human Capital. They should start by discovering such citizens even from the university level and then move on to provide them with all the recourses required, as well with nurturing and motivation along with motivation bonuses so that the highly-qualified citizens may thrive creatively. Besides, a Nation's well-being depends heavily on the intelligence, the knowledge and the decisions of those people. It is also unquestionable that the contribution of the latter is to be acknowledged with a view to further enhance their willingness to provide more creativity-induced services not merely to their own Nation but to the Humanity as a whole.

I now wish to elaborate more on the methods of psychological war employed by the hegemonic State against foreign States. Specifically, those methods share affinities with the ones commonly used on psychological war (be they known or unknown), yet, at the same time, they have been modified so as to be effective on the individual level, in accordance, that is, to the personality and the psychological traits of the individual they wish to destroy.

3.8.1. Methods employed for either the Diminishing or the Erasure of the progression of Scientific Research & Innovation.

It is possible that a hegemonic State focuses its efforts on hindering either the National or/and the global recognition of excellent and to a large extent maverick scientists belonging to its controlled state. They do so through the control they exercise on the information (see e.g. the gatekeepers in both scientific activities and in the Mass Media). The rationale behind all this is that a hegemonic State wishes to retain its dominance and the financial as well as status and power-related benefits this dominance brings along. More specifically, let us consider the case when praiseworthy scientists publish their articles: distortions of fundamental concepts and keywords are possible; reference numbers in the bibliography pertaining to breakthrough discoveries can be altered, thus causing confusion and corrupting the name, the appreciation and the intellectual propriety of the author. Indeed, the corruption of the author's name deprives them of their right to receive credit as the authentic creator of an original scientific research article. Equally possible is the falsification of words appearing in the article thus distorting its spirit and the omission of keywords and phrases that seriously compromises textual effectiveness. Of particular mention is the use of another tactic, namely the initial acceptance for publication, only that this publication date gets deferred *ad infinitum* – so much so that the article's author finally ceases to inquire about the publication date altogether. Similarly, there are cases where there is a very long delay in the publishing of the article in an internationally renowned journal, until a different article on the same topic receives publishing approval in some other scientific journal. Additionally, it is worth examining how in example, even registered mail (mine) containing potentially publishable work fails to be delivered to an international scientific journal (e.g. an oncology journal); also, how, on account of conflicting interests an original article fails to receive the green light for publication (e.g. on an article that foresaw the causes – for instance an administrative incompetence – of the third most serious nuclear accident and which, incidentally, was very well received by the scientific audience[13]). Likewise, the common reasons given for turning down an article for publication leave a lot to be desired in terms of persuasive power: instead, what is typically given is either the reviewer's decision or old excuses such as 'typographic errors are to be attributed to ... some 'demonic agent' . Now, a sophisticated method of curtailing the prominence of scientific, business and other cutting-edge on an international level ventures is the Internet's most popular search engines' reluctance to place them in the foreground. It becomes obvious that depriving scientists and their important work of exposure is a method of IDW which works in favor of, say, other states, that incessantly and in various ways promote, via the whole range of the Mass Media, their own scientific institutions and the scientists whose work serves those states' agenda.

Very Critical for the scientific Researchers and the Humanity is that "Those" who control the publications in major scientific journals and in the major mass media communications often they Block Independent & Unknown Excellent scientists to publish their Fundamental ! scientific research. However in some cases they may allow the publication of "minor details" research and so they force those Excellent unknown & independent scientists to publish their ideas and Fundamental research f.e. in Internet, from where very easily "they" can steal the unknown & independent scientists' research, for the interests & benefits of very advertised institutions & for the mass media controllers own interests & benefits...(This is a personal experience of this author,f.e in his Very Critical scientific research in Nuclear Safety(f.e. [13],[39]), in Fundamental Theoretical Oncology(f.e. [38]) and in other fields of science(references his CV with the attached CD of July 2014,[36] & Elsewhere)...

3.8.2. Impediments to the creative development of excellent scientists and to the flourishing of scientific activities.

When scientists become overly specialized whilst this tendency of theirs to delve exclusively into scientific over-specialization is encouraged at the same time, and also when, in conjunction with all the above, the dominant trend is to show esteem for scientific research with criteria that are based on 'production quantity' (e.g. a plethora of publications) rather than on 'discovery quaity', then the overall result is suffocating deadlines, excessive labor and the narrow-mindedness of otherwise eminent scientists. The latter refers to the fact that scientists can't see the wood for the trees. In other words, they study a minute segment of reality, namely, they focus on their over-specialization and thus overlook the 'whole picture' of realty. Most importantly, THIS attitude blocks some really important 'brains' of the scientific sphere from getting involved with the robust aspects not only of the human existence but also of science/technology – and all this because of a **significant lack of available free time save from time spent on super-specialization**. Thus, this is an **IDW** method because it distracts the finest scientists and renders them indifferent to the substantial and vital issues that Humanity faces.

I now wish to discuss another war tactic against Intelligence, one that it is employed so that Nations are deprived of any potential benefits that may spring from excellent scientists begins right after the latter's graduation from tertiary education. More specifically, during the time of their military service most often (due to IDW) serve either as soldiers or as sergeants and then their personalities and character are subjected to downright humiliation by practically illiterate non-commissioned officers and officers alike [5]. This is a pattern of behavior which derives from the influence of foreign powers that take advantage of military officers' psychological complexes (mainly their egotism) so as to push for the introduction of military laws according to which Excellent scientists must serve, statistically, as mere soldiers or sergeants (and extremely rare as officers) [5].

Furthermore, when the controlled State offers meager financial rewards and no recognition to its 'high intelligence and knowledge' sources (e.g. to the fine scientist and the like) whereas, by contrast, the so-called 'hegemonic' States offer towering financial and other rewards to fine scientists, this incongruence results in the well-known phenomenon of <brain drain> [28] that seriously affects the controlled States, not least because of the fact that their eminent scientists migrate to the hegemonic State permanently (let us also bear in mind here that the hegemonic State's foundations rely heavily on the motto 'Knowledge is Power'). Once they settle to the hegemonic State, the scientists in question enjoy recognition whilst, at the same time, the controlled States remain subjects and mere customers of the hegemonic State, thus powerless to give birth to state-of-the-art scientific and technological achievements. Another ramification of the 'brain drainage' phenomenon and of the State's deprivation of power brains in particular is that, when it comes to the controlled States the crucial job posts and key decisions are under the jurisdiction of mediocrity and perhaps at the hands of individuals who are either implicitly or explicitly, very susceptible to the influences of foreign interests (since more often than not they even fail to realize the presence of such interests – perhaps unsurprisingly so, as this is a skill that requires apt intelligence and equally acute awareness skills. In this way, the National interests of the yielding States face long-term, medium-term and short-term extinction – in which case we are talking about IDW targeting a human organization (i.e. the State).

The author of the present study is the mastermind behind the theory called 'A theory on the evolution of an intelligent ecosystem', which significantly modifies the Darwinian theory of evolution in the context of an ecosystem and thus to render Darwin's theory even more relevant to our era of high intelligence/knowledge and technology. The theory in question was published in the scentific journal of the Association of Dutch and French Theoretical Biclogists 'Anta Biotheoretica', 45 (2), June 1997, p. 181-182 and in the author's web address which was the following: www.ncmr.gr/Kondylakis.html.

Very malicious interests stopped latter the operation of this author's Internet site and also stopped, twice, for years, the operation of his professional email communications in his work (HCMR, Greece). They blocked his telephone and fax communications with the Aristotle University of Thessaloniki, Greece (from which he has graduated with "Excellent" degree), stopped his emails & fax communications with the Physics Dept. of McGill University, Canada (from which he has postgraduated with a Canadian Scholarship) & stopped his communications elsewhere. Also, with a huge violation of the European Treaty(ies) in the European Parliament, during last years, the Petition Committee of European Parliament do not register his Petitions to European Parliament, even when many of his Petitions are concerning Vital Themes such as: the International Nuclear Safety & Security[39], Fundamental Theoretical Oncology scientific research[38], Control of Humanity, E.T.C. (and his relevant actions for help to European Ombudsman(s) and to European Union Court resulted in unfair results), and also illegally they block/stop this author (a Nuclear Physicist) communications with the main telephone and fax of the International "Atomic"(NUCLEAR!) Energy Agency (I.A.E.A.)E.T.C... [36].

3.8.3 Psychological/Psychiatric war against individuals of high intelligence and knowledge as well as against individuals in vital job positions.

CIA (the USA's premier secret information service) is the pioneer in research on 'Mind Control'. It can be argued that what started it all was the program called MKULTRA, which was launched in the early 50's. Ewen Cameron, a CIA agent, and Professor at McGill University (Montreal, Canada), is thought to be a mastermind behind it. Cameron collaborated with the CIA on a series of psychiatric studies – among which there were studies related to 'psychic driving', etc. [7],[8],[9],[12],[22],[24],[29],[30]. A basic concept on 'mind control' of eminent personalities (top scientists, diplomats, military officers, journalists and the like) revolves around the practice of emitting at the auditory threshold of an individual (and also in locations such as their workplace, their residence as well as in their hotel rooms and their vehicles) various scenarios/stories with a goal to cause intrusion to his/her thoughts, thus leading them into believing that all the stimuli are the product of their own thinking; the ultimate aim is the management of perception in terms of event(s) interpretation. In other words, this manipulation enables its instigators to implant the desired evaluation of events in order to facilitate the afflicted individual's perception skills and behavior. The afore-described method may be used in conjunction with hypnotizing techniques and, as a consequence, through the combination of implicit [10] and post-hypnotizing orders so that their plan for human 'mind control' become more effective. Only the imagination of those who exercise human control can put a halt to the consequences of this method that are so far-reaching that may even lead to premeditated suicide or 'accidents'. Additionally, in cases of scientific, industrial and military espionage they can– again through the emissions at the auditory threshold–extract information and ideas from their target (especially if this person has not become aware of the technique in question); alternatively, techniques from the fields of psychology/psychiatry are employed to enforce collaboration: more specifically, they may emit a question and then may ask the person to slightly nod their head either to the right (in case the answer to the question is affirmative) or to the left (in case the answer to the question is a negative one).

In addition, it is possible that ideas and interpretations of facts that shape the individual's conception of reality, both well-researched by psychologists and psychiatrists, crawl into the individual's conceptual framework by means of the previously described methods. For instance, one method of industrial espionage involves the secret services of sophisticated industry-wise States recording conversations between top scientists in premises such as restaurants, Universities as well as their private talks in conferences [18]; Also, the recording is even feasible in private residences. The overall aim is the stealing of the finest ideas so that they may later implant them into the auditory doorstep of eminent scientists living in their own State, thus speculating those ideas as their own; thus, they succeed in pioneering at scientific research and publications as well as in technology and economy of their own State. By contrast, the original creators of the idea are bound to find serious obstacles in both the reception and implementation of their ideas. In a similar vein, as it is known from the press [19], a vast amount of electronic services is being tapped mostly by the USA, thereby making it possible for the secret services of the hegemonic States to spy on scientists and to also make the theft of scientific articles possible through personal computers that are connected to the INTERNET. It is also possible to create personality and research interest profiles of the scientists in question because of their accessing and stealing of information and keywords that have been stored in the scientists' internet –connected personal computers. Thanks to the access gained to the scientists' computers the hegemonic States can perform an analysis of behavior patterns, their interests (i.e. through credit card records, mobiles telephones information, computer usage patterns) and the like [17], [31]. Indeed, it is officially announced by the European Parliament [33] that ISDN landline telephones in homes, companies and other organizations have the potential to record conversations taking place in the vicinity of said landlines, **even when the receiver is well-placed in its proper position** – this is deemed possible through the emission of a monitor signal. In other words, surveillance on the part of American services based on the USA is technically viable thus violating both the privacy of intimate and family conversations in the worst imaginable way.

In addition to the aforementioned points, there has currently been an extremely critical and well-informed debate, accompanied with the relevant countermeasures, regarding the imminent introduction from USA-based companies of operating systems for personal computers connected to the INTERNET. Now, in order for the personal computers to work, it will be mandatory for their owners to submit – in full - their personal data to the company which acts as an operative system provider. Consequently, the company will be in a position to pilfer all the readily available information (records, e-mail and e-mail contact lists, programs and so on and so forth) at any given moment from all of the personal computers, and on a global scale at that, since the latter's function is dependent on either the said operating systems or on various other INTERNET communication programs (browsers, cookies, etc.). Moreover, this pilfering of information may take place automatically while the worldwide incessant theft of information may supply an enormous basic data management system with perpetual updates and, accordingly, distribute this information whenever the basic shareholders, CEOs of these companies (the government of the USA included) wish to do so.

Of equally fundamental importance with regard to personal data protection and Human dignity is the future introduction of the so-called 'interactive TV' wherein all Human beings using it around the globe **will be fully monitored by specific companies right from early childhood**, and this close monitoring is bound to involve the detailed and on a daily basis recording of the individuals' interest(s) in (space, time, case), hobbies and personality traits followed by the classification of the findings in temporal-spatial basis and in accordance with each individual case. Similar may happen from Internet search computer programmes, as f.e. the Google, e.t.c.

In the above-described cases, namely Computer operating systems and Interactive TV, though this is also pertinent to other cases as well, the companies collecting the data then move on to **the meticulous structuring of user's personality profile, which is updated daily and may subsequently be used for both the implicit and/or explicit exploitation of Human and humanly operated Organizations (States, Private companies and the like). Similar happen from Internet search programmes as the Google and others.**

I should now warn the reader against using any communicative devices (telephone, Fax, Computer etc.) designed in or originating from the USA, because they are designed in such a way so that the said State may watch all received and sent information by the user's device – this is, after all, in compliance with 'The FBI Bill' [17], the USA law signed by President Clinton on the 24th October 1994.

All these problems touch upon fundamental Human Rights and, as any International Convention can secretly be violated by the Hegemonic States, we argue that the systematic and in-depth research on and studying of these problems is an urgent desideratum. On the European Union level, defense mechanisms against this tactic as well as against similar ones could include both the stricter legislation and the effective implementation of relevant legislation along with the simultaneous support of the Organizations which are subject under both State and European Union control thus aiming at the creation of computer programs that will be operating in a safe functional system as well as secure internet Browsers and internet search engines; equally crucial is the development of safe deciphering systems for electronic mail including for other essential computer programs. Moreover, what needs to be vehemently stressed is the fact that, because of the realistic possibility [33] of the theft of information not only from American organizations and businesses but also from other States – a prospect that is tantamount to the snatching of priceless scientific, financial, Stately and many other cutting-edge activities (let alone the profiling of the European citizens etc.)- the issue in question must be made well-understood and lucid to the European Union states and be treated as one of (the) highest priority for the launching, among other measurements, of relevant scientific research programs, studies as well as for the creation of legislation (including its ensuing effective implementation) along with technology and raising the awareness of the body of citizens on the topic under discussion.

Likewise, diplomats and armed forces officers are likely (for instance during the period of their further training in a foreign State and the like) to receive, through emissions at their auditory threshold, internalized ideas and interpretations of events. Ultimately, the individual potentially regards these ideas as their own, thus their perception management is shaped according to the interests of the foreign State. As a result, those individual's decision-making acts linger on the avenues and behaviors desired by the foreign state. Additionally, because of the said method of perception manipulation, the individual may, through psychological tactics adapted to their own personality, be convinced of irrational perceptions of reality, thus leading them to either madness or/and to the onset of temporal psychotic states.

The afore-described technique of the individual's perception management may work in combination with the emission of microwave electromagnetic speech radiation that directly targets the brain (on the scientific viability of this theory, see, inter alias, [11], [12], [15], [16], [23]) thus making the individual feel that they have been 'hearing voices' – a situation that, to the uninitiated medical staff may be considered as a pathological condition. There are apt examples of eminent scientists with integrity and with the best of intentions who emigrated to a hegemonic State or to a state under the control of a hegemonic one either for postgraduate studies or for employment and who, perhaps even unbeknownst to them, they were reduced to mere guinea pigs for the hegemonic State's financial, scientific and other interests.

It is a well-known fact (e.g. [8]) that psychological/psychiatric methods might be used in order to relinquish the influence and the social recognition of the dissident voices and of those who are able to both become aware of and make known to the public the disastrous plans deriving from hegemonic or totalitarian States.

A very effective way of destroying the cognitive Intelligence of a Human(s) is by using psychiatric methods (often with institutionalization in psychiatric clinic),including psychiatric drugs, also given to children i.e. to hyperactive children(who, incidentally, are, quite often, the most intelligent children) and the illegal (or made legal?) use of narcotics drugs, made available in high-intelligence places as Universities, Schools and also in bars, streets and elsewhere and advertised in...TV usually in "music" and films, and various other 'artistic' representations...

3.8.4. Psycholinguistics and its Impact on the Intelligence Destruction War

The majority of the readers are familiar with case-studies wherein someone merely says way too much without their words having any essence; the same applies when someone reads a plethora of pages of a written text without them learning anything of substance. These cases are referred to as IDW techniques and are also employed by a segment of the Mass Media of States for National or/and international influence.

The crumbling of exactitude in speech, as well as the destruction of wholeness and of the succinctness in expression, serve to withhold the dissemination of the basic principles, concepts, and themes – they are also yet another IDW technique.

The usage of words that strike a discordant note because they do not promote the logical progression of the text, thus hindering exactitude (words as 'inserts') is a very harmful IDW technique of the Mass media, one that it is exhaustively used in highly advertised magazines and in other printed material in the Mass Media and in TV so that they exercise psychological pressure to the reader. The author of the present study has come to the bitter realization that the very same technique is almost ubiquitous in many scientific textbooks and terminology handbooks, even though they have been authored by CEOs in nuclear energy organizations.

The corruption of the true meaning of words and the impoverishment of language from words that stimulate intelligence use or, in a similar manner, the minimization of the usage of such words, constitute IDW. To exemplify this, let us consider a realistic intelligence usage test that involves watching people conversing with each other, whilst you estimate the frequency of the use of the following words: a) 'BECAUSE' (for introducing logical reasoning) b) WHY (for introducing logical criticism) c) 'Does this have the sense of...' (for introducing scrutiny and critique of the reason(s) given). Indeed, one will be truly taken aback by the negative results testifying to the intelligence of a public residing in a hegemonic State – apparently, the latter is at pains to keep its citizenry in the lowest possible level of critical reasoning statistics-wise, so that citizens can be intellectually (or mentally) controlled by the Mass Media in particular and the state-induced information flow in general.

Altering the emotional tone of certain words by associating them with different emotions than they usually connote is quite likely to viciously affect not merely the person's emotional world (it can ever trigger pathological states) but, in extension, their intelligence as well [15].

The use of highly materialistic terms and words (a very common practice in the USA) may significantly curtail the theoretical advancement of sciences as well as of creativity in terms of the introduction of new fundamental concepts, of philosophy and all of the intellectually higher discourse in general. All this too is an IDW technique. For, no Human evolution is feasible through materialistic recognition and rewarding alone. Should we wish to talk about long term evolution, then the recognition and rewarding of the non-materialistic goods should also be sought for.

By the same token, modifying the precise meaning of words (e.g. 'look how hot it is!', instead of the correct 'can you feel how hot it is?) may result in mental confusion, and thus act as an IDW technique.

This author has also heard from TV a former rector of University specialized in... linguistic to say "I see" instead of the correct "I understand", etc ...

Furthermore, the linguistic analysis of the logical reasoning as the latter appears in a written text or a transcript could act as a method of evaluating the author's intelligence (assuming, of course, that the appropriate written text and topic have been selected to this end).

3.9. Violations of Justice against Creative Intelligence Individuals.

By subjecting individuals who have creative intelligence to violations of Justice which are a source of incessant hardship(through, for example, thefts, robberies, abuses, destruction of both mobile and non-mobile property, slander, frauds, forgeries, lying under oath as well as excessive noises and other malignancies in the workplace or/and in the private homes, injustices, deliberate red tape, refusal to provide services, payroll issues, and other justice violations) – this whole network of hardship makes the life of the individual who is endowed with creative intelligence unbearable – so much so that their intelligence is impossible to thrive, while at the same time those individuals are forced to become involved in projects that are not germane to their own projects (in other words, we are talking about distraction from creative work). As a result, all the afore-mentioned violations of Justice constitute a method of IDW, the ulterior motive of which is to drain the repository of the person's abilities and intelligence.

3.10. Disastrous activities on behalf of both secret services and services related to private organizations.

Both known and unknown methods of psychological war – and of war in general – might be used by States 'secret services, probably alongside with international and/or local organizations (both secret and obvious ones) that are affiliated to them; the same might also be the case with private clubs that are influential enough to inflict catastrophic problems (IDW) on anyone who refuses to succumb to their agenda, thus ultimately distracting them from their main occupation and causing, through the constant hardships, a deficit in the efficacy of their intelligence. There needs to be national legal protection with a view to combat the afore-described ramification that seriously harms the National Human 'capital' (i.e. human resources of highly creative qualifications etc.). In the era of the European Union, the term 'National' is also construed in accordance with the long-term, medium-term and long-term interests of the European Union.

3.11. Catastrophic propagandistic strategies

Amongst its many roles, propaganda can also prove a useful weapon of destruction of one's social reputation and status. Now, with regard to the State in question, the Mass Media quite frequently ignores the individuals who have been bestowed with high intelligence and an impressive knowledge pool. Very often revolutionary ideas or/ and expressions with their reasonable arguments are not allowed to be expressed by the mass media communications or by oppositional political party(ies) or by the law or others. This may include political cases, racism cases, accused cases, non-standard scientific theories, conspiracy theories, e.t.c. In this observation they are very relevant the famous saying of Voltaire "I disapprove of what you say, but I will defend to the death your right to say it" and that the first goal of Justice and Science is to finding the real Truth...

By way of exemplification, one could mention here from the mass media communications the erasure of stellar scientists in almost all scientific fields (with the exception of medical scientists). By contrast, what it is promoted ad nauseam are the sources of stupefycation (such as singers of the worst imaginable quality as well as of actors who propagate idiotization and lose morals).

As a result of the afore-mentioned ICW tactics, the citizenry is manipulated into being interested in, discussing and being solely engaged in topics of very low intelligence and also in trivialities (this is, incidentally, a form of counter-education offered by the Mass Media; it is so against-education, that it both obliterates and overturns the audience's formal education), while, at the same time, constructive discourse on topics relating to both creative intelligence and useful knowledge suffers a terrible blow. Additionally, the social recognition of both highly intelligent and highly knowledgeable (University Professors, top scientists and the like) individuals dwindles and what is maximized instead is the social promoting of the making the people stupid, sources as astrologers, football players and the like.

It is also known that the Mass Media's propagandistic tactic of presenting the extreme exception of a rule as *the* rule results in the disfiguration of reality – worse even, the Media constructs a disastrous reality that smashes the reputation and violates the trust in the State's creative institutions, thus leading to the destruction of social recognition and respect towards the individuals who serve those institutions; in effect, what is encouraged is the formation of an environment that is utterly unfavorable to the use of creative intelligence. Some typical examples include the shaming of Justice and Religion by means of the exploitation on the part of the Media of isolated cases that constituted an abuse of duty and violation of creative morality.

3.12. Catastrophic impact on the institution of the family and on constructive Religion

"Give me better families and I will give you a better world"
(Archbishop Christodoulos)

A highly effective IDW method that targets a sentient man involves interfering in this man's family. More specifically, the interference purports to cause family rifts and eventually even the wrecking of the family. The very same method has, in the past, caused even highly creative for serving the State's interests Prime Ministers (e.g. in Canada) to be made inert.

The wrecking of a family home is concomitant with a series of psychosomatic as well as practical problems. In turn, these problems act disastrously upon the individual's motivation for getting involved in highly intelligence and knowledge matters. Conversely, a harmonious and nurturing family environment not only fosters humanitarian interests but also optimizes the potential for activation of intelligence, of creativity as well as of the impulse for creative work.

Statistically speaking, one rather quite effective tactic for instilling familial conflicts (if not inducing the complete dismantling of interpersonal relationships) includes the high emphasis given by the Mass Media to the vast number of methods that are conducive to the emergence of interpersonal problems, while simultaneously promoting as viable only those solutions that ultimate destroy interpersonal bonds between people. For example, the exaggerated underscoring and the psychological easiness which contribute to couples' quarrels alongside the re-naming of loose morals as 'cleverness' in both TV soap-operas and printed material whilst, concealing, at the same time, any co-operative and creative suggestion for resolving the conflict for the family's own good. Among other destructive interests is the desire for financial gain, as a family that has been torn apart is perhaps a more welcome consumer than the close-knitted one (consider, e.g. the needs for purchasing new appliances, cr the morey paid on recreation that aims at finding a new partner and so on and so forth). The discussion in the scientific article [6] further elaborates on a role (a main interest of those who control the Mass Media communications) of the Mass Media in the dismantling of interpersonal relationships and for Family destruction...

In order for a fecund environment which will favor the development and use of intelligence to be created, the Naticn, the Mass Media, and the employment Organizations need to correspondingly cultivate an environment that will foster creative social relations. By way of example, we may consider North America: for decades now, the Universities, Research Institutions, and all employment agencies as a whole have been placing great importance on the social activities of employees (e.g. banquets, dancing events, discussion groups and the like), thus contributing to the increase of employment productivity. By contrast, the terrorism exerted by Mass Media through the news and films only brings about social isolation.

Another IDW tactic concentrates on the demolition of constructive Religion. Specifically, the tactic in question is actualized by Mass Media productions which bully both people of faith and delegates of constructive Religion (i.e. Christianity) as has been dictated by those who control the Mass Media either directly or/and obliquely. Now, by definition, constructive Religion confers upcn the believer Love, Good Hope, and creative faith and it therefore contributes, through its creative moral outlook, to the enhancement of societal relations and to a better quality of life. It also acts as a psychological 'life saving' in times of despair and may even avert psychosomatic illnesses, encourage recovery from diseases (a fact also corroborated by the medical science) and even prevent people from committing suicide. In statistical terms, the Religious individual's perception management is directed towards the building of a better future and it precisely because of this intellectual outlook that all too often they do 'discover' the better future. Consequently, statistically speaking, they are happier than those who lack the aforementioned benefits bestowed by creative Religion.

3.13 Other IDW methods

There is a multiplicity of methods for the destruction of intelligence – so many, in fact, that only the imagination and knowledge of humans may contain them.

4. Countermeasures Against the Destruction of Intelligence War

The cardinal countermeasure against the IDW is that this war to become fully understood and perceivable by those who have the overall responsibility to deal with the whole matter, so that all appropriate measures for the protection of the Nation, the citizens, and the human organizations affected or potentially affected by the IDW may be taken.

The next stage involves both the formation and the ensuing efficient function of the right infrastructure of organizations both in Nation and the European Union level that will subsequently prompt an analysis of IDW in terms of both its principles and practices, followed by an in-depth analysis of specific case-studies with a view to forge successful defense mechanisms against IDW that will be valid in short, medium and long – term. To this end, it is imperative that interdisciplinary committees be formed consisting of Scientists, technology experts, as well as medical scientists (e.g. medical doctors, psychologists, and psychiatrists); the committees in question must also include scholars from the fields of Law and Ethics, as well as of Public Relations and Military Science and Technology; finally, the contribution of scientists from the fields of Management and Motivation in Organizations and Mass Media is required.

The overall concept informing the creation of countermeasures against IDW must revolve around the scrutiny of possible modes for Intelligence Destruction along with the discovery of methods that will force the latter to become unrealizable, or at least, to devise ways that will minimize the damage caused in short, medium and long-term to both organizations and to the Individual.

Due to the serious scarcity of coherently published literature on the present topic, the main aim of the current study is to establish a solid background – by means of an overview of some intelligence destruction methods (some of which, regrettably, the author has experienced as victim…), for the enhancement of scientific research aiming at the introduction and implementation of legislation, adherence to the legislation in question and finally at case-law and decisions in both the National and European Union levels which will be acting as countermeasures to IDW.

Another particularly effective defense mechanism against IDW involves the European Union, the Nation, and other employment agencies becoming actively involved in a discourse that will be seeking to find and subsequently efficiently benefit from highly intelligent and knowledgeable individuals by simultaneously providing them with the fitting motivation and motivation rewards including the relevant resources. It is to those individuals that all means disposable should be directed at, along with ensuring that the former will be allotted with the appropriate natural and psychological milieu as well as facilities, security, and recognition, so that the possibilities for optimum decision-making on their part gets maximized in accordance with spatial, temporal terms for each particular case that can be of concern to the European Union, the Nation, and the organization. What should be made transparent is that nowadays only the motto 'Power in Unity'- in the sense of the synergy within the European Union, wherein the result from the sum of collaborative efforts can be much higher than the sum of the supposedly independent (read: Nation's) ones – coupled with the motto 'knowledge equals power'(when talking about the future) – a policy that the USA has been espousing as one of utmost long-term priority given their urge to hold on to their preponderance and exclusivity in information - can lead us to happiness. Last but certainly not least, these two mottos aside what can guarantee our happiness is the optimum development of the 'high intelligence and knowledge sources' in both National and European Union levels in conjunction with further research, study, and resistance against IDW.

5. Conclusion

The life-affirming message is that the potency of critical, high cognitive intelligence and relevant information, human decisions, the pertinent knowledge and the originality can at times obliterates the systems' standard operation procedures and can all prove to be so powerful and even win a resounding victory over military equipment costing trillions of dollars – especially when they spring from the concepts of Morality and Justice.

We firmly believe that what must become both clear and commonplace is the fact that the long-term creative development of an intelligent ecosystem in our planet [20] will only be rendered possible on condition that any fundamental and determining of Humanity's future decisions are both scrutinized and taken by inter-scientific committees consisting of stellar individuals endowed with creative intelligence and knowledge whose sense of creative Justice and Morality has been established. Those committees will be studying the impact of all areas of both knowledge and types of activity. It thus emerges clearly that all resolutions of the said committees should be amply justified not only in terms of reasoning but also in terms of constructive emotions: they must be predominantly based on logical democracy [21], not on the servicing of negotiation interests.

Finally, with regard to the dissemination of information to the public via the Mass Media, under no circumstances should information violate the principles of Morality and Justice as these have been laid out by the International Principles of Human Rights so that what can ultimately emerge is a better quality of life for future societies from the standpoint of Health, Family, Morality/Justice as well as the standpoint of Ecosystems, Culture, Science/Technology, Economics, creative interests, leisure time and other parameters. On the concept of Human Rights we must be very careful to imply constructive natural entities and not to misused...

Note: This author has been experienced very strong IDW in his life in Greece,Canada and in European Union...

6. Acknowledgments

The author wishes to thank Professor A.G. Andreopoulos (Rector at the Technical University of Athens, Greece), Dr. Christos Anagnostou, Mr. Panayi Georgiou, Ms. Theodora Karvouni, Dr. Alexis Konidis, Dr. Theodoros Kousouris, and last, but certainly not least, Dr. Efi Kotou for their constructive criticisms and valuable comments.

7. REFERENCES

[1] The Fundamental article "The constructive intelligence as legal value" by Joseph-Christos Kondylakis, published in the Greek Law Journal "Criminal Justice',October 1999, from page 1055

[2] The Fundamental article "A model on the structure and operation of memory from the view of intelligence" by Joseph-Christos Kondylakis, in National Library of Greece, 1982

[3] The Fundamental article "A contribution of theories of information and mathematical logic" by Joseph-Christos Kondylakis & Georgia Sakarellou, in the proceedings of B Conference of Greek Ad-

ministration Judges, in Athens, Greece, on presentation of 2-December-1990, from page 162

[4] "Destruction of Intelligence and High Treason" by Joseph-Christos Kondylakis,in National Library of Greece,1997

[5] The Fundamental article "The factor of (cognitive) Intelligence in the armed forces and its correlation to the spirit of criminal justice" by Joseph-Christos Kondylakis,published in the Greek Law journal "Yearly edition Armenopoulos",1999, from page 141

[6] The Fundamental article 'Media effects as a factor of breaking close relationships', by Joseph – Christos Kondylakis, National Library of Greece, 1999

[7] 'The Search for the Manchurian Candidate: The CIA and Mind Control: The Secret History of the Behavioral Sciences' by John Marks, 1991. Norton Press

[8] "Anti-political psychiatry" by Dr Kleanthis Grivas,publisher Ianos,Thessaloniki,Greece,1989

[9] The Fundamental Books 'Opinion of John Cooper, Q. C. Regarding Canadian Government Funding of Allan Memorial Institute in the 1950's and 1960's (*Prof. Ewen Cameron CIA Brainwashing* Experiments at McGill University in Canada), edition of Department of Justice in Canada, Ottawa, Ontario, Canada K1A0H8 and 'I swear by *Apollo: Dr. Ewen Cameron* and the *CIA-brainwashing* experiments', by Don Gillmor, 1987, Eden Press

[10] The Fundamental book 'Hypnotic Realities' by Milton H. Erickson et al, 1976, Irvington Publishers

[11] "Biological influences of the electromagnetic radiation " by Prof. K.Th. Liolousis,1997,publisher Diaulos,Greece.(In its pages 51-53 is presented the possibility of causing cardiac arrest and in its pages 55-56 is presented the possibility of transmitting "voices" directly to the human brain, in both above cases by using pulsing microwaves radiation).

[12] "War for the Destruction of Intelligence and Legal Protection" by

Joseph-Christos Kondylakis, 2002,in National library of Greece (and also exist relevant law action of this author to the Prosecution of the Supreme Criminal Court of Greece).

[13] The Fundamental article "Some Uncommon but Very Critical Aspects of Nuclear Safety" by Joseph-Christos Kondylakis, submitted for publication to journal "Nuclear Engineering & Design" and it received very good scientific comments from its chief editor Prof. Jacques Poirier,Commisariat a l' Energie Atomique (DRN) France, but other bad interests blocked the publication of my Original and Very Critical article in this journal. However this author received for this article a warm thankful letter personally signed from the President of European Parliament Madame Nicole Fontaine. This very critical article was also sent to the International "Atomic"(NUCLEAR) Energy Agency, but they did...not reply to this author...

[14] "Thinking on the basic equation of work performance" by Joseph-Christos Kondylakis,published in the Greek newspaper "Kathimerini of Sunday" on 15-October-2000, page 74

[15] The Fundamental article "An influence of semiotic to psychology and psychiatry" by Joseph-Christos Kondylakis,Very Original scientific article,in National Library of Greece and in the archives of psychiatric journal "Psychiatry" of the Hellenic Psychiatric Association,2018 (It is considered by the Hellenic Psychiatric Association remarkable, but it was not published in the above journal because of its many pages). This article was published (via my Internet site that contained my many pages scientific article) in the official scientific journal of All-Greece Medical Doctors Association the "Iatriko Bima", issue 84, in 2003, in its section "Medicine On-line".

[16] 'The Zapping of America: Microwaves, Their Deadly Risk, and the Cover-up', by Paul Brodeur, 1977, Norton Press

[17] 'The end of privacy' by Charles J. Sykes, 1999, St. Martin's Press

[18] 'Confidential' (Spying on Science & Commerse) by John Nolan, 1999, Harper Business Publication

[19] 'Big Brother NSA& its Little Brother' by *Terry* L. Cook, 1998, SCM Publishing

[20] The Fundamental article 'Theory of Evolution of an intelligent eco-system' by Joseph-Christos Kondylakis, *Acta Biotheoretica, 1997, 45 (2),pp. 181-2.*

[21] *'Logical Democracy' by* Joseph-Christos Kondylakis, National Library of Greece

[22] 'Psychic Dictatorship in the U.S.A.' by Alex Constantine, 1995, Feral House Publishing

[23] The Fundamental article 'Auditory perception of radio-frequency electromagnetic fields', by Chung-Kwang Chou and Arthur W. Guy, *The Journal of the Acoustical Society of America*, June 1982, pp. 1321-34

[24] 'Psychiatry and the CIA: Victims of Mind Control' by Harvey M. Weinstein, M.D., American Psychiatric Publishing, 1990

[25] 'Motivation and work behavior' by Dr. Richard M. Steers et al., 1996, McGraw-Hill

[26] *'Media* Effects: Advances in Theory and Research', by Jennings Bryant (edt), 1994, Lawrence Erlbaum Associates Publishing

[27] The Fundamental book 'Human Factors in Engineering and Design', by Dr. M. S. Sanders et al., McGraw-Hill

[28] «The Knowledge revolution- an analysis of the international brain market», by Dr D.N. Chorafas, 1968, McGraw Hill

[29] «Mass control: Engineering Human consciousness», by Jim Keith, 1999, IlluniNet press

[30] "Technology for enslaving conscience " by Dimitris Euaggelopoulos,2000,publisher "Esoptron",Greece

[31] *Corporate espionage* by Ira Winkler, 1997, Prima Publisher

[32] Internet site: www.ncmr.gr/Kondylakis.html

[33] "Development of surveillance technology and risk of abuse of

economic information" (98/14/01), frcm *European Parliament, Scientific & Technological Option & Assessment.* Internet site: www.europarl.eu.int/stoa/publi/default_en.htm

[34] Additional relevant scientific articles are available at the following INTERNET address: www.ncmr.gr/Kondylakis/index.html (Later bad & illegal interests and actions stoped the operation of my Internet site)

(Addendum)...

[35] The information that follows is germane to our theme: my lawsuit to the General Prosecutor's Office of *Areios Pagos* (Supreme Court of Greece) with protocol number 8081/5 November 1998; additionally, my lawsuit to the District Attorney of the Public Prosecutor's Office of First Instance Criminal Court in Athens, Greece with protocol number IB2010/6120; see also my folder to the *Greek "Atomic" (NUCLEAR) Energy Commission* with protocol number 8800/ 5 July 2017.

Also investigate for the Big Problems & Barriers put to this author' scientific research and life in Greece,Canada,Europe...

[36] From my communications with the Crim nal Prosecutions of [Supreme Criminal Court of Greece, Second instance Criminal Court in Athens, First instance Criminal Court in Athens], the Royal Netherlands Embassy in Greece, *EURATOM* (and the author's victory in European Commission competition COM/A/301 in 1980 as qualifying as a Nuclear Installations Inspector), the International "Atomic" (NUCLEAR!!) Energy Agency, the International Criminal Court,also in this author Petitions (those of Not-registered! and those of registered) to European Parliament and Elsewhere... Also some additional information exist in my writings (under my user name "Petition" and "Thinking") in the Internet site : https://semfe.gr/forum/viewforum.php?f=21

[37] (Added latter in 2018): A relevant interesting book is entitled "Your Thoughts Are Not Your Own: mind control, mass manipulation

and perception management", by Neil Sanders, Two volumes, 2013

[38] The Fundamental(meaning defining new direction(s) of research) Theoretical Original scientific research entitled "Unified Theory of Oncology" (which may act as a "compass" to Guide & accelerate the applied oncology scientific research towards to probable cure of cancer disease,e.t.c.) by Joseph-Christos Kondylakis. My first main article was created in 1983 and then further developed and a summary of it was presented in the 7th European InterUniversity Symposium on "Recent advances in Diagnostic imaging and Supportive Care in Oncology", on 17-20 July 1997 in Thessaloniki,Greece. Later my main article was published (by using my Internet site that contained my many pages scientific article) in the official scientific journal of All-Greece Medical Doctors Association the "Iatriko Bima", issue 84, in 2003, in its section "Medicine On-line". Now part of my scientific research exist in the Internet, in my relevant Petitions to European Parliament (registered and not-registered Petitions of mine) and more information exist in the Royal Netherlands Embassy in Greece, in my C.V. with its attached CD of July 2014 and Elsewhere...

[39] The Fundamental first Quantitative! scientific research entitled "Theoretically and under very special applied conditions a Nuclear fission reactor may explode as Nuclear Bomb" by Joseph-Christos Kondylakis,published in the proceedings of 19th scientific symposium of the Hellenic Nuclear Physics Society,held at the Aristotle University of Thessaloniki,Greece on May 2010,also it exist in Internet site: http://inspirehep.net/record/1441083/files/Fulltext.pdf

SUPPLEMENT

"Criminal Justice" Greek Law Journal of issue
October 1999
CRIMINAL JUSTICE
MONTHLY EDITION
FOUNDER – DIRECTOR: Jacob I. Farsedakis
EDITORIAL BOARD:
George Arbanitis Former Deputy District Attorney in Areios Pagos (Supreme Court of Greece)
Antonis D. Maganas, University Professor
Jacob I. Farsedakis, University Professor

Regular Contributors

Eirini Athanasiou, Lawyer, Postgraduate Diploma in Criminal Justice, University of Athens, Greece

Stergios Alexiadis, Professor

Antonios Astrinakis, Assistant Professor

Candido Da Agra, Professor at Porto University, Portugal

Dimitrios Vlasis, Lawyer, UN Crime Prevention and Criminal Justice. Vienna

Pierre-Henri Bolle, Professor at UniversitédeNeuchâtel, Switzerland

Jacques Borricand, Professor at Aix-Marseille University, France

Henry Bosly, Professor at Louvain University, Belgium

Willy Bruggeman, Assistant Coordinator Europol Drugs Unit; Doctor in Criminology & Statistics, University of Brussels

Kyriaki Grigoriou, Member of the Council of State,DEADroit Public Paris I

Maurice Cusson, Professor at the University of Montreal, Canada

Nikolaos G. Dimitratos (PhD). Lawyer

JanVanDijk, Director of Strategy Research, Ministry of Security &Justice, the Netherlands

Christina Zafonitou, Assistant Professor

Andreas Zygouras, Deputy District Attorney at The State Court of Appeal, Greece

Umberto Gatti, Professor at Genova University, Italy

Panagiotis Kaisaris, Deputy District Attorney at The State Court of Appeal, Greece

Petros Kokkalis, Supreme Court judge

Dimitrios Kalogeropoulos. Emeritus Director of The National Centre for Scientific Research, France; Professor and Director of the Centre for the Sociology of Law & Justice, University of Brussels, Belgium

Lambros Karampelas, Associate Professor, District Attorney at The State Court of Appeal, Greece

Ilias Kastanas (PhD), Lawyer, Researcher at the Marangopoulos Foundation for Human Rights (MFHR)

Nikolaos Koulouris, Doctoral candidate in Criminology

John Ktistakis, Lawyer (L.M.M.). DEA Political Sciences, Researcher at the Marangopoulos Foundation for Human Rights(MFHR)

Efi Lambropoulou, Assistant Professor

Aikaterini Matsa, Psychiatrist, Scientific coordinator of the Drug Rehabilitation Centre at the PHA

Gaetan DiMarino, Professor at the Aix-Marseille University, France

George P. Nikolopoulos, PhD in Criminology, lawyer

Emmanuel Nonas, Forensic Medical Examiner A', Chief Medical Examiner in Forensic Science Division Service, Athens

Pelagia Papazaxariou, Professor at Columbia University, USA

Eustratios Papathanasopoulos (PhD in Law), Deputy District Attorney at the Court of First Instance of Athens

Theodoros Papatheodorou, Assistant Professor

Agapios Papaneofytou, Assistant Professor

Haris Papacharalampou, Lawyer (PhD in Law)

Haralampos Poulopoulos, KETHEA Director

George Rigas, Supreme Court Judge

Francesco Sclafani, Professor at the University of Napoli, Italia

Eugenios Trivizas, Professor at Reading University, UK

Aglaia Tsitoura, former Director at the Criminology Division at the Council of Europe; Professor Emerita, University of Brussels, Belgium

Ioanna Tsiganou, (PhD in Law) National Centre for Social Research, Greece

Olga Tsolka, Lawyer (PhD in Law)

Irvin Waller, Professor; General Director of the International Centre for the Prevention of Crime(ICPC), Montreal, Canada

Andreas Fakos, District Attorney at The State Court of Appeal, Greece

Anthozoi Xaidou, Associate Professor

Creative Intelligence as a Lawful Good*
(*alternative translation:
Constructive Intelligence as Legal Value)

In our sensory world, everything is dependent upon natural laws, 'chance' as well as upon human and animal decisions.

The conclusion to be drawn from the aforementioned parameters is that human's intentional impact on either an earthly or an unearthly environment is associated with both decision-making and the implementation of those decisions. Consequently, the choice of a set of targets that it is appropriate for the temporal-spatial needs coupled with the optimum implementation of this set of targets, is directly correlated both with human intelligence and human organizations' intelligence.

The optimum realization of a set of targets converges on optimum both spatially and temporally decisions. By **Optimum Decision,** one refers to such kind of decision that maximizes the possibility for the realization of a series of targets both spatially and temporally, yet simultaneously safeguarding that any existing restrictions in relation to the set of the targets will be obeyed.

By the **Basic function of a Mathematical Set**, the members of which are dependent on certain factors, one refers to the correspondence electing the set of those factors which to the maximum degree affects the parts of our initial set.

By **Human Intelligence** we refer, in the present study, to the process of solving scientific, social, legal etc. problems and/or to the non-random choice of an optimum solution pertaining to a decision-making problem by means of an algorithm which might include a series of logical processes, such as the iterative question process (*Why? Because, Does it have the sense of?*) on the causes that need to be understood [1], [2],[3] .

By **Intelligence of Human Organism**, we refer to the effectiveness in problem-solving, wherein problem-solving comprises of the making of the optimum solutions in spatial-temporal terms and their ensuing execution. The intelligence of Human Organization is fundamentally correlated with the intelligence of the individuals who form part of the Organization, the structure (e.g. hierarchy, committees and the like) as well as with the networking of decisions, the information available and the quality of those decisions. It is also correlated with the psychological environment and the resources available. As the borderline case of human organization's intelligence we may consider the scenario where the organization consists of one individual only, thereby we are talking about **Human Intelligence**.

By **Creative Intelligence** we refer to the type of intelligence that offers creative solutions to problems. Specifically, it contributes either to the preservation or to the creation of order and harmony in specified systems. Viewed under this light it may also share affinities with the phenomenon of the decrease of entropy in a thermodynamic system [2].

Within the framework of contemporary times, especially the modern 'Risk Society'(*Risikogesellschaft*) [4], the concept and function of the Lawful Good itself in those new circumstances and, by keeping in mind Birnbaum's [5] formulation that virtues include either 'people or things', we assert that the definition of Intelligence should be ranked among the critical human attributes. This is also supported by cognitive psychology [6], [7]. To sum up, the afore-described argument alongside the concept of creative intelligence that was analyzed above and in conjunction with the fresh definition of Law proposed in articles [2], they all lead one to think of creative intelligence as a Lawful good in an evaluative sense.

The fundamental principle of respect to and protection of Human Worth (c.f. Article 2 of the Greek Constitution), yet also the overall protection of lawful order and the State's Creative evolution are directly dependent upon both Creative Intelligence of Humans and the Creative Intelligence of the human organizations that have been partaking in the aforementioned activities. In this respect, the importance of safeguarding the virtues of Human Creative Intelligence and Human Organizations' Creative intelligence must become obvious.

Cases of war for the destruction of creative intelligence have been recorded in both the International Relations [8] and Public Interest domains [9]. In other words, individuals or/and organizations, possibly including states, attempt to bring other individuals or/and organizations, possibly including states under their own control. The reasons for doing so are financial, national as well as religious, political and so on and so forth. Consequently, it becomes transparent how urgent it is to call for the heavy criminalization of said practices.

The term 'Intelligence Destruction War' refers to the destruction of Human Intelligence and/or of the Intelligence of the Human Organization; the destruction in question might be owed either to malicious or criminal negligence be it partial or total, a temporary or a permanent one (the aforementioned War might take place in the level of natural persons, legal entities, Nation and State. In its ominous form, we argue that the said War can culminate in treason crimes against the Nation as well as in High Treason [10].

The reverberations of the destruction of an organization's creative intelligence via, for instance, selecting individuals of low creative intelligence in pivotal employment positions through to the destruction of the social set of creative intelligence (following the indirect manipulation of its behavior – through, in other words, the *'robotization'* of humans) via destructive productions by the Mass Media may be proved to be fatal for the State in national, international [11] as well as financial, cultural, social and other levels.

Examples of Practices for the Destruction of Intelligence include the following:

1. Lack of motivation and lack of rewarding motivation for the fostering of creative intelligence.
2. A shortfall of or destruction of the quality of knowledge provided (in education and the information world).
3. A deficit in or a destruction of organizations' creative hierarchy (absence of meritocracy, immorality and the like).
4. Harmful Mass Media productions.
5. Working and living ecosystems that are damaging to creative intelligence.
6. Disastrous state policies (bureaucracy, time-consuming procedures, special favors, nepotism and the like).
7. Remunerative legislation that is damaging to creative intelligence.
8. Psychological/Psychiatric interferences in both the individual and the collective mindset.
9. Law offenses against individuals with creative intelligence.

10. Calamitous activities of secret services anc related privately-owned services.
11. Calamitous propagandistic tactics.
12. Catastrophic effects in the family, creative religion and the like.

In stark contrast to non-Greek literature, very seldom does the issue of lawful protection of creative intelligence appear in Greek bibliography. Be that as it may, since the Seconc War World onwards, there has been a rekindling of state concern in facilitating and protecting – in the broader sense of the term- the pioneers (even from college level) and the eminent scientists in the developed States, and particularly this is in the State's major priority for crucial aspects of economic, scientific and military interest (e.g. maverick IT, genetics, nuclear physics, medical scientists and in general for all modes of major scientific, technological and cultural innovation in general).

Given all the afore-analyzed discussion points and, taking into consideration the global paradigm of the developed States, it is fair to say that, in order for a State to survive and subsequently thrive in the International sphere, it is imperative that it sets at the top of its agenda the employment of all its protective mechanisms in order to provide safe refuge for the creative Intelligence of both its cit zens and its humans organizations' own.

By Joseph-Christos Kondylakis
Nuclear Physicist/Information Technology Expert

BIBLIOGRAPHY

[1] Joseph-Christos Kondylakis "A model on the structure and operation of memory from the view of intelligence", 1982, in the National Library of Greece-based

[2] Joseph-Christos Kondylakis & Georgia Sakarelllou "A contribution of theories of information and mathematical logic to the improvement of offering Justice", in the proceeedings of B Conference of Administrative Judges,Athens, December 1990, from page 162

[3] J.-C. Kondylakis, 'Theory of Evolution of an Intelligent Ecosystem', *Acta Biotheoretica, 45 (2)*, 1997, pp. 181-182.

[4] U. Beck "Risikogesellschaft, Auf dem weg in eine andere Moderne",1986,in Kourakis N. (editor) "Anti-criminal politics',Athens,1994 (article by N.Dimitratou "Views of modern problematization in the theory and practica of criminal law",page 142,note 3)

[5] Birnabaum, 'Über das Erforderniß einer *Rechtsverletzung zum Begriffe* des Verbrechens, mit besonderer Rücksicht auf den *Begriff* der Ehrenkränkung', Archiv des Criminalrechts, Neue Folge. 1834, p. 149-194.

[6] M.W.Eysenck & Keane, M.T. 'Cognitive Psychology: A Student's Handbook (6th Ed.)'. Florence, KY: Psychology Press, 2010

[7]. Haberlandt, K. *Cognitive psychology* (2nd ed.). Needham Heights, MA, US: Allyn & Bacon

[8] J C Goldstein, *International Relations,* Hamper Collins Press, 1994

[9] A. I Taxos "Law of public order", publisher Sakkoulas,1990

[10] Joseph-Christos Kondylakis "Destruction of intelligence and High Treason",1997, and note on his article of 9-December-1997, in National Library of Greece.

[11] A. Papadamakis, "Violations against the international status of State", publisher Sakkoulas,1995

THE WAR AGAINST INTELLIGENCE FROM A CRIMINAL JUSTICE PERSPECTIVE

Josef-Christos K. Kondylakis. Greek Center for Marine Research.

Wednesday, 15 January 2003. Postal Code: 19013, Attica. Fax no: 22910-763223

Abstract: The present paper is a scientific research study which, drawing on the author's previous work ('Intelligence as a Lawful Good' (1999), 'War of Intelligence's Destruction and Legal Protection' (2000) and 'Intelligence Destruction War' (2001)), purports to establish within a theoretical and practical discourse framework the **vital** need for both Nation and Welfare State to activate mechanisms predominantly of Law protection, but also other relevant mechanisms that will act against the destruction of both human and human organizations' cognitive intelligence – not least because of the fact that the quality of decision-making processes is correlated with the status of the aforementioned Intelligence – in extension, the well-being of the Nation and the **quality** of life of the citizenry is also affected.

Intelligence Destruction War refers to the destruction of Human Intelligence and/or of the Intelligence of the Human Organization; the destruction in question might be owed either to malicious or criminal negligence be it partial or total, a temporary or a permanent one (the aforementioned War might take place in the level of natural persons, legal entities, Nation and State. In its gravest form, the author believes that the said War can culminate into treason crimes against the Nation as well as High Treason [Kondylakis, 1999; Kondylakis, 1997].

'Intelligence of the Human Being' refers, in this study, to the capability for problem-solving (scientific, military problems and the like) and/or to the **non**-random choice of an optimum solution pertaining to a decision-making problem by means of an algorithm which might include a series of logical processes (such as the iterative question process: *Why, Because, Does It Have the Sense of?*) on the causes that are to be understood.

Due to the fact that the IDW compromises the ability for rational decision-making and because, either treacherously or via criminal negligence, it stupefies Humans and/or Human Organization, the Intelligence Destruction War against Human(s) or/and Human Organization may, among its other repercussions, result in the following:

1. Destruction of the lawful good of Human(s)' HEALTH (namely Greek (Criminal) Penal Code – Crimes against life (Chapter 15 of the Penal Code). Also: Penal Code – Bodily Harm (Chapter 16 of the Penal Code)

2. Destruction of Scientific Potential (namely Penal Code – Crimes against health {as above (1)}. Penal Code – Crimes harming the honor (see Chapter 23 of the PC) of a Scientist and Nation's Treason (see Chapter 2 in PC) in special circumstances, i.e. in cases where our Nation's respected and creative scientists are destructed – with all the repercussions involving poor quality and harmful decisions for both our Nation and our citizens' well-being.

3. Financial destruction of Person(s) or/and Human Organization(s) (that is to say, PC-Crimes against proprietary rights (see Chapter 24 of the Penal Code) as well as Crimes against Proprietorship (see Chapter 23 of the Penal Code) and numerous relevant articles in the Civil Code etc.

4. Individual Destruction of a person/or persons or/and Human Organizations (that is Penal Code – on harming a Person's Worth and Health, etc.)

5. Social Destruction of a Person/Persons. (that is Penal Code – on harming the psychosomatic health (in both the Social and Individual plane, Destruction of Family life, and the like; also see more related articles in both Penal and Civil Code, etc.).

6. Destruction of the Person(s)' individual freedom either through oblique means (via reduction of the Psychosomatic capabilities and of Human health {for instance by rendering the individual imbecile or through their unwilling enclosing into a psychiatric hospital (often used for dissident individuals) or convincing them to remain contained in an enclosed environment, and the like}, or direct means (for instance by a restraining order after forcing– because of DW– the person into obtaining one or through unwilling enclosure in psychiatric hospital, a practice often used for dissident individuals and, as a rule, expressed as an order and not as well reasoned intelligent diagnostic decision on cause(s) of the case.)).

7. Destructions in various other fields (see relevant Penal Code articles, Civil Law as well as the pertinent to the matter legislation of both Greece and Foreign States by bearing, of course, in mind the correct and relevant to IDW interpretation of said legislation, etc.

In his 2002 study 'Crimes against life and health' (Mpekas, 2000), John Mpekas asserts that in chapter 15 of the Penal Code entitled 'Crimes against life' and in chapter 26 of the same document entitled 'Bodily Harm', **_health_** is to be defined as a protected lawful good (page 23 ibid.).

What is more, Mpekas defines the term 'health' as the temporally specific condition of physiological, **bodily or/and mental (psychological) functions** of the Human Organism. On page 23 of the aforementioned study, Mpekas then goes on to argue, quite plausibly in our opinion, that, should this condition be disturbed (even for a **minuscule amount of time**) or should **any** of the previously described functions be either **thwarted**, rendered non-viable or even force the body to activate a process of emergency resuscitation by any type of behavior, then this behavior causes health harm.

(from a scientific standpoint, we feel the obligation to commend John Mpekas on the exceptionally accurate and comprehensive definition he has provided us of the term 'health harm' – not least because the term in question belongs to a wider discourse that is in itself quite problematic in its articulation on an international level).

The suggestion that in both Chapters 16 ('Bodily Harm') and 15 ('Crimes against life') of the Greek Penal Code (PC), the concept 'bodily' harm {based on the teleological interpretation which is also considered to be the correct interpretation of Justice (see, for instance, Tsatsos' study titled 'Interpretative problems of Law') is employed in order to exemplify somatic or **/ and psychiatric harm** against health and life, gains further support from the following: 1) the lawmaker's causal expository report, wherein there is a special consideration for viewing crimes from a psychological outlook (c.f. A. Kontaxis, Sept. 1997, p.41) in view of (the findings of) recent studies in the fields of Anthropology, **Psychology**, all previously predominant views on crime); c.f. also A. Kontaxis, Sept. 1997, p.48: 'in our contemporary times, criminal justice sciences form a complex nexus of knowledge that considerably exceeds the older, finite limits of Criminal Justice Law. Anthropology, Forensics, Psychiatry as well as Biology, Sociology, Medical Examiners and Statistics are merely one part of this cycle of sciences that invite the judge to be well-versed in.' Additionally, in Kontaxis, 2000, Vol. B., p.2575 'among the harm on health embedded are the conditions pertaining both to bodily and **mental health'**. This thesis stems from article 310 according to which bodily harm is likely to beget a threatening medical condition for either the body or the cognitive abilities. Likewise, as 'Harm on health' is defined as **any** condition involving either somatic or **mental health** or even **aggravation** of a pre-existing pathological condition. As health harm is also understood **every** etiology or accentuation of a disease (for example, when one is incapable of making **sophisticated** decisions due to, to name one reason, administration of strong psychoactive drugs or to Electroconvulsive therapy(ECT) (causing impoverishment of associative memory, tremor, and the like); another reason may also be the cognitive MURDER resulting from lobotomy – all these interventions are destruction of intelligence methods) irrespective of the time span of the said condition.

Any harm on mental health is always to be seen as synonymous of inflicting harm on one's health (see also Margaritis, p. 159; Phillipidis, p. 179; Gafos, d97′, and also as a result of interpretation originating jointly and teleologically from PC3 10, etc.).

With reference to the 15th chapter of the Penal Code, we contend that a distinction is in order, one that distinguishes between two forms of **Death**, which in terms of the Penal Code hold equal weight. More specifically: A) **Bodily Death** (e.g. failure of vital brain cells that are instrumental in the continuation of life); and B) **Psychological Death** (**e.g.** types of **psychiatric LOBOTOMY**, irreversible coma or any other adverse events inducing a person to a 'vegetable state'.

To the extent that the **Intelligence Destruction War (IDW)** negatively affects the **value** of decisions involving *in concreto* situations, it might even lead to PSYCHOLOGICAL DEATH (e.g. by means of psychiatric methods) and to BODILY DEATH (e.g. by means of malicious actions as well as by leading the person in a moronic state, and subsequently employing the method of murder by 'statistical death traps' as it is a case with certain avenues where the green light for pedestrians is **very often** out of order {e.g. in the vicinity of *Greek Center for Marine Research* in the Aghios Kosmas area). In a similar vein, there have been cases where the pedestrian is hastily attempting to catch the public bus in a bus stop that has been placed in the most dangerous location thus making it very likely for a fatal car accident to occur. By way of illustration, one could refer here to the bus stop for the 'A2' bus in the area of Neon Faliron, despite the existing safer alternatives for the installation of a bus stop spot.

The Intelligence Destruction War affects not only the quality but also the degree of Human decisions' efficacy, although this influence varies among individuals. Supposing a splendid scientist is destroyed via IDW, so that he is capable of making decisions solely on manual tasks (e.g. on how to create 'a work of art' in a mental institution). In this case, we are talking about a serious harm, as this is eloquently discussed in Mpekas' s brilliant study entitled 'Crimes Against Life and Health': 'Thus, the control exercised on life and health (2002, p. 24) thus, the assessment of how seriously one's health has been attacked is NOT to be based upon any predetermined and fixed threshold; in fact, what the assessment must take into consideration is the REPEATED comparison of one's health condition PRIOR to any intervention (e.g. PRIOR to the administration of psychotic drugs, electroshock therapy or LOBOTOMY or other psychological/psychiatric impact on the Human Being; by way of analogy, by examining how the ACCOMPLISHED Scientist would perform in both Scientific and other activities, and the like). Likewise, the assessment must take into account the behavioral outcome POST intervention, where perhaps the ACCOMPLISHED Scientist is deemed 'fit' to perform only manual 'work-therapies'...

Compared to the excellent scientist who, as we have already mentioned, undergoes a kind of INTELLECTUAL DEATH (which is tantamount to a PSYCHOLOGICAL DEATH) due to the implemented Psychological/Psychiatric measures (either in the negative sense of the term or by a FRAUDULENT manner), a RESPECTABLE agriculture worker, PERHAPS???? would even dig his own land MANUALLY – as a result of the administration of either psychotic drugs, electroconvulsive therapy (or the MURDER OF HIS OWN PSYCHE brought about by LOBOTOMY)...

The author of the present study maintains that the INTELLIGENCE DESTRUCTION WAR, a war that first and foremost invalidates or stop the 'WHY? -question' for issues of behavior or events (c.f., for example, the methods of **passive** listening advocated by Sigmund Freud, an overtly-advertised by the Mass Media man of Jewish descent and so-called 'father 'of psychology/psychiatry), is to be regarded as one of the MOST EFFECTIVE ways of INTELLIGENCE DESTRUCTION WAR. This is clearly supported in a twofold manner: first, by the very definition of the term 'Intelligence' that was provided at the beginning of the present study (namely enquiring about causes, n-iterative cycles {WHY?, BECAUSE... DOES IT HAS A MEANING?}, etc.); and secondly, by the cardinal importance of intelligence for the degree of quality and efficacy of Understanding and of Human decision-making and the latter's' ensuing consequences for the Human Being(s), Society, Humanity and Intelligent Ecosystems.

Note: "The Protection of (cognitive) Intelligence in the Law of Personality and in the Civil Justice" by Joseph-Christos Kondylakis,2019

In the Greek law book ("The Law of Personality" by Karakostas John,2012) in its page x (index) we can add the additional element of personality which requires legal protection "4. The cognitive Intelligence [Kondylakis, J.C.,2001]", as an element of personality, which as such is justified from the definition of personality(read above mentioned book of John Karakostas, pages 47,48) .Also it must be put this element of personality(cognitive intell gence) ir John Karakostas' book chapter XII.2 about the protectior of emotional and mental health of personality.

Additionally,probably,in a wider meaning,we car think about the protection of (cognitive) Intelligence of an organization (read at the beginning of this book of J.C. Kondylakis the definition of intelligence of a human organization), under the meaning of a legal personality.

BIBLIOGRAPHY

Kondylakis Joseph-Christos "The constructive intelligence as legal value", published in the Greek law journal "Criminal Justice", October 1999, pages 1055-1056

Kondylakis Joseph-Christos "Destruction of intelligence and High Treason",1997 and his note on this article of 9-December-1997, in National Library of Greece.

Joseph-Christos Kondylakis & Georgia Sakarellou "A contribution of the theories of information and mathematical law to the improvement of offering Justice" in the proceedings of B Conference of Greek Administration Judges, December 1990, from page 162

Joseph-Christos Kondylakis "War for the Destruction of Intelligence and Law Protection ",2000,in National Library of Greece-based

Joseph-Christos Kondylakis "War for the Destruction of Intelligence",2001, in National Library of Greece-based

Joseph-Christos Kondylakis, "An influence of semiotic to psychology and psychiatry", 19-February-2002, in National Library of Greece and in the archives of journal "Psychiatry" of the Hellenic Psychiatric Association as, and it was existed in Internet site : www.ncmr.gr/Kondylakis/psychiatry.html

Mpekas G. "Crimes against Life and Health",2002,publisher Sakkoulas

Kontaxis A. (editor) "Criminal Law" of Greece, September 1997

Kontaxis A. "Criminal Law: Interpretation",volumes A + B, 2000, Greece

Karakostas John, "The Law of Personality",2012,publisher Nomiki Bibliothiki.

INTELLIGENCE DESTRUCTION
AND HIGH TREASON

Josef-Christos Kondylakis, 1997
Nuclear Physicist/
Information Technology expert

'Intelligence of the Human Being' refers in the present study to the capability for problem-solving (scientific, military problems and the like) and/or to the non-random choice of an optimum solution pertaining to a decision-making problem by means of an algorithm which might include a series of logical processes (such as the iterative question process: Why, Because, Does it has the Sense of:) on the causes that are to be understood [1],[2],[3]..

According to the Penal Code (henceforth PC), in Article 134, Section 2, the term 'Violence' may, in accordance with the lawmaker's intent, to be also interpreted as psychological manipulation of Human(s). This is an all too necessary interpretation (in the sense of the capacity for optimum decision-making) for the normal function of a human and the system of government.

By 'system of government' is meant the organized form of the State. [5]. 'State' is construed as the uniform phenomenon of the organized (i.e. without disorder or anarchy) social coexistence of the people. [5] Now, characteristics of the 'State' [5] include the following parameters: a) the country b) a social body c) state organization and d) a primordial form of power.

From the afore-mentioned arguments, it derives that a prerequisite for 'normal function' is the normal function of state organization and this consequently sets as a prerequisite the protection against either its infringement (anarchy) or deformation (Mass Media). Added protection is required against rendering state organization inactive, as it is the case with the War on Intelligence.

Nevertheless, given the fact that article 2 in Section 1 of the Greek Constitution regards the protection and respect towards the Human worth as the State's primordial duty, it results from the holistic Conceptualization of Justice as a complete and contradiction-free whole, [4] that, in order for the optimum protection of the Human worth to be materialized in spatial and temporal terms in the Greek state it is compulsory to optimally utilize the sources of Intelligence + knowledge+creative-*cum*-fair mental state (Creative Intelligence) both inside and outside Hellenic jurisdiction. For this reason, any destruction of the Creative Intelligence sources, irrespective of the means of said destruction, mostly on a long-term, yet also on sort and medium-term, leads to non-optimum, and even damaging to human worth decisions (in conjunction with the damage imposed on their mental and physical health on both the individual but also the statistical level of the societal whole, etc.); alternatively, any destruction of Creative Intelligence sources renders the democratic regime partly inactive (e.g. psychological manipulation by the Mass Media of the executive, judicial and legislative function of the State, either/or the destruction of society's Intelligence); additionally, it is equally possible to either witness the normal function of the democratic regime undergoing a mutation to a state of anarchy or to destroy the very core of the state (e.g. war waged on the part of secret services for the destruction of intelligence by means, say, of **exiling creatively intelligent people away from Greece or by obstructing them from taking over posts that are crucial for the development and well-being of the country; also by engaging in a psychological war aiming at their demise, and so on and so forth).**

Because of all the afore-mentioned reasons, we argue that the destruction of creative intelligence of the Greek Nation constitutes an act of high treason (PC Art. 134).

A Note added in later years by Joseph-Christos Kondylakis :

The War for the Destruction of (cognitive) Intelligence is very possible to exist, at least in statistical form and for special individual cases, against almost all nations of Humanity, in which case we must think about a Crime Against Humanity (ref. [6], [7]) .

This may be justified because any purposeful human action depend on only two factors: the human' available information and his/her cognitive Intelligence. Therefore if his/her cognitive Intelligence is destroyed then the Human can be telecontrolled as robot, f.e. from mass media communications (including the Internet)... It can also be considered as Crime Against Humanity when the War for Destruction of Intelligence can serious effect the International Nuclear Safety or/and Security or other Vital Themes of Humanity or/and planet Earth ecosystems.e.t.c.,...

BIBLIOGRAPHY

[1] "A model on the structure and operation of memory from the view of intelligence" by Joseph-Christos Kcndylakis,1982, in National Library of Greece.

[2] "A contribution of theories of information and mathematical logic to the improvement of offering Justice" by Joseph-Christos Kondylakis & Georgia Sakarellou, in the processing of B Conference of Greek Administration Judges, December 1990, from page 162.

[3] 'Theory of Evolution of an intelligent ecosystem' by Joseph-Christos Kondylakis, *Acta Biotheoretica, 45 (2),pp. 181-2*, June 1997

[4] "The problem of interpretation of law" by Konstantinos Tsastos, 1978

[5] "Elements of Democratic Politic' by Peristeropoulos B, Giannakopoulos P. and Karalis A, published by the Greek Ministry of Education (Organization for publication of Educational Books), 1991

[6] "Commentary on the Law of the international Criminal Court " by editor Mark Klamberg, TOAEP publisher, 2017

[7] "Relevant communications of Mr. Joseph-Christos Kondylakis with the International Criminal Court, Criminal Prosecutions in Athens,Greece, Royal Netherlands Embassy in Greece & Elsewhere

A FEW NOTES ON THE ARTICLE ENTITLED 'DESTRUCTION OF (CREATIVE) INTELLIGENCE & HIGH TREASON AGAINST THE NATION'

Josef-Christos K. Kondylakis
9 December (12) 1997

In accordance with the lawmaker's intent, which is substantiated by historical research (e.g. 'A Report of the General proposal on the Parliamentary Committee on Justice' (rapporteurs: Mr. V.Stefanopoulos, Mr. H.Logatos; Committee Chairperson: Mr. N. Mpalopoulos)

[page 41 in {1}]: 'In the light of novel research in the fields of Anthropology, **Psychology,** and statistics....'

[page 48 in {1}]: 'In our time, Penal Sciences constitute a large nexus of knowledge which to a large degree exceeds the older and rigid boundaries of Penal Justice. **Psychology** in particular,....'

It emerges that is was both the spirit and intent of the lawmaker that the topics germane to the Destruction of Creative Intelligence of our Nation to be included in the PC 134 and – in broader terms- in the second chapter of the PC (Penal Code) on Treason against the country. Thus, the topics in question are viewed as a true legal lacuna that is to be supplemented; hence, in teleological terms, all the above justify our interpretation of the term 'Violence' in PC 134 and in the Second chapter of the Penal Code as follows:

(a term that ALSO) includes THE PSYCHOLOGICAL MANIPULATION OF HUMAN(S) THAT RELINQUISHES THE ABILITY FOR OPTIMUM DECISION-MAKING IN BOTH SPATIAL AND TEMPORAL TERMS AS WELL AS IN INDIVIDUAL CASE-STUDY/IES.

BIBLIOGRAPHY

[1] "Penal Law" of Greece, editor Kontaxis A., June 1997

[2] "The problem of interpretation of law" by Prof. Konstantinos Tsatsos,1978

ON COGNITIVE INTELLIGENCE PROTECTION
LAW ACTIONS

Everything in our sensory world is dependent upon natural laws, 'chance' as well as human and animal decis ons.

From the aforementioned factors, we infer that human intentional influence exerted on either the Earth or to non-Earthly ecosystems directly depends on Human decisions and the execution of those decisions. Thus, there is an imperative need for the choice of the optimum decision(s) in (space, time, case) – so that the set of desired goals to be achieved. Here is where the parameters of Human Intelligence and of the Intelligence of Humans' Organizations come along (cognitive 'intelligence' is **not** to be confused with the term 'information' here).

More specifically, the meaning of 'Human Intelligence' in the present study adheres to the definition provided in the author's contribution to the *Future of Europe Debate* (eventuated at December 17, 2001) in his intervention entitled *Human Intelligence + Education+ Religion in the Future of Europe.* In a similar vein, the definition of 'Intelligence of Human Organization' may also be found in the author's article 'Creative Intelligence as a Lawful Good' (written in Greek), published in the Greek Law Journal *Poiniki Dikaiosini (Criminal Justice; October 1999 Issue*, pp. 1055-1056).

In contemporary times, actions, as well as events and facts observed, lead us into arguing that a Destruction of Nations' Human Intelligence (and also of constructive/creative emotions) is well under way.

Specifically:

1. In many nations (USA, EU, and others), the Mass Media propagate the view that we should only be 'doers' and not 'thinking human beings' (with the meager exception of their encouraging of the existence of automated, common thought patterns). It is a true fact that in many nations there is animosity for discussions which de-

mand thinking (there may exist only descriptive talks, the majority of which are in essence a replica of discussion patterns of media productions). In short, the human model of the 'doer' for the 'mass of the people' is favored over this of the 'thinker', so that the controllers of mass media to "telecontrol' the Humans... Possible proof may come from the simple scientific intelligence use test, as this is described in my contribution to the *Future of Europe Debate* (as above), titled 'RE: Media Culture + Human Intelligence + Emotions (paragraph 3)/Thoughts on the multi-cultures of European Union" linkage, or mentioned in this book paragraph 3.8.4. "Psycholinguistic...".

2. The Media productions in Greece and perhaps in other countries, too, continuously advertise and air (by allotting considerably maximum air time) the...astrologists, the mystics, etc. – this is only for the likes of Idiots and ultimately these are productions which turn the public into an idiotic and controllable one. What is more, the MONOTONY in restricted space and the repetitive events such as football & basketball games inflict TIREDNESS AND TORTURE to THE INTELLECTUAL MIND (it is quite degrading for the mind to just WATCH the athletic game and very different from the benefit from the GYMNASTICS that PLAYING the actual game offers). In Greece today, seldom will one hear discussions from, say, University Professors (except medical doctors) or from genuine intellectuals; instead, one will be continuously watching (and NOT thinking) astrologists, football players and possibly cinema actors discussing and proposing "solutions" to contemporary problems.

3. It is the opinion of the author that scientific publications from excessively advertised USA universities are of much inferior quality COMPARED TO the publications written before the 1950s. This could possibly due to the fact that back then the scientific thought had not yet been contaminated, as it were, by both media productions and the noise that advertising creates to the human mind. Mod-

ern terminology on 'computer science' and mathematics strongly echoes the … economics terminology, rather than this of natural sciences, that was in use before the 1950's.

4. The majority of children today are forced to listen to narratives (stories, etc.) that are, in our opinion, destructive for their intelligence and their constructive/creative emotions.

5. Compared to the past, recent graduates from Education Institutions (and the educational system in its entirety) has not well developed, statistically speaking, both the reasoning and thinking abilities of their students (the same too probably applies for the teachers themselves). When it comes to Greece, in particular, we feel that the major reasons for this are the Lack of motivation (while there exists a strong ANTI-MOTIVATION mood), (which consist of lack of financial and other kinds of incentives) for the students as well as teachers and graduates. Case in point: an elementary school graduate in Greece (e.g. a house builder and the like) is likely to earn ten times more money than a holder of a post-graduate degree does. And this may even result in the poor quality of the culture produced in the country (e.g. the so-called *skyladika* = *dog barking-sounding* and, by implication, *dodgy* songs; the fashion style that promotes black as the ultimate fashion choice that is tantamount to promoting the mood of funerals; the uncivilized behavior; the degrading of the Greek philosophical diction and language, etc.).

6. The Greek Mass Media productions very often promote the exception to the rule as *THE* rule, thus causing a deformation of reality and the latter's distortion for the presentation of worse (in cases, for example, of the performance of Justice Officials and Religion Priests and the like).

7. E.T.C.

Because of the above and

B1. Given the arguments presented in the article written by the author and titled 'Constructive Intelligence as a Legal Value'/'Creative Intelligence as a Lawful Good'

B2. Given the United Nations' Human Rights Conventions Articles 1,26 (paragraph 2), 30.

B3. Given the *Charter of Fundamental Rights of the European Union* [CFREU] articles 3: (paragraph 1) (because the Human intelligence is part of mental integrity); 24 (paragraph 1 & 2), 26 (because most information to disabled Humans comes through Media productions and so the latter must show respect for Human Intelligence and not destroy it), 51, 52.

B4. Because of the Greek Constitution Articles 2 (paragraph 1), 7 (paragraph 2), 14 (paragraph 1 in conjunction with the Criminal Law), 15 (paragraph 2), 24 (paragraph 1), 25 (paragraphs 1+2+3).

B5. Because of the Greek Criminal Law articles:

308, 309, 310, 312, 306

FOR ALL THE REASONS MENTIONED ABOVE and perhaps for additional other reasons

We may recommend to the European Union Nations to think and act for the Legal protection of Human Intelligence (and constructive/creative emotions)

s.n: This contribution may be brought about and may be used from public prosecutor(s) of any Nation(s) for public protection...

REFLECTIONS WITHIN THE PHILOSOPHY OF JUSTICE FRAMEWORK

Josef-Christos K. Kondylakis

13 May (05) 2003. Contact number: 22910-76322

(author's relevant copyright submitted to *E.A.P./8081 5-11-1998*)

A. On definitions germane to the concept of 'Justice'

1) 'What is Justice? The term **Justice** refers to the **knowledge** about the allocation of an immaterial or/and material good (yet also of something which is not deemed 'good', as in the case of sentencing) to a totality of people who belong in the set {1 2....N}, wherein N equals a positive integer number. Ideally, the said allocation contributes to the **optimization** of the psychosomatic or/and material status of both individual AND the set of people, towards **a creative trend** (à)

(N.B.: an original definition of Justice that is the most implementable one in practical terms is to be found in the scientific research by Mrs Georgia Sakarellou,Judge at Administrative Court in Greece and Mr. Josef-Christos Kondylakis,Nuclear Physicist [1]).

2) **Justice** refers to the offering of Justice spirit in concreto case(s).

(**Note:** The Justice (and the Justice spirit, a fundamental virtue) may be different from Law(of certain interests).

3) As **Justice/Correct** is defined the sentient being whose knowledge is related both to Justice spirit and to the virtue and sciences that are related to the Justice spirit for the offering of Justice. The sentient being in question has a predilection for ('virtue', according to Aristotle [2]) correctly **offering** the Justice

4) **Optimizing** refers to the **process** of determining the farthest (this is usually the maximum or minimum, but we tend to ignore any saddle points) within system(s) of equations or/and inequalities,

whilst safeguarding, **simultaneously**, that the **systems' restrictions** will be maintained.

B. Justice & Constructive Ethos (for instance of CHRISTIAN (Orthodox) Religion)

1) The etymological basis of the word **Ethics** is the Greek word *ethos*– the latter is a longer type of the word *ethos* which denoted **habitual or customary conduct** [3]. To be sure, morality is not tautological with habit, although it would be correct to argue that they share affinities, due to the fact that habitual behavior fosters and strengthens morality [3]. (P.S.: This is due to the conditioning of behavior psychology).

Thus, '**ethos**' may also allude to human behavior patterns as well as dispositions, expressions, and their manifestation. All these are solidified, as it were, through habit and finally determine the individual's personality [3].

Constructive Ethos denotes the ethos that generates order and harmony in the ecosystem.

Now, **Christian anthropology** situates Man in an angle of boundless personal freedom, one which extends far beyond any material, biological as well as a social or secular necessity. Man is God's creation. The constructed and destructible man is traced back to the *aktistos* (incomposite, uncreated, hence without beginning or end) and eternal God, who is the equivalent of Love [3].

Christian Ethics are founded upon the principles of Christian anthropology [3], the most important of which are **freedom** AND **Love** that permeate orthodox Christian ethos. The **unyielding spirit** and **selflessness** hold a very special place in the Christian tradition and they may be considered to be the empirical manifestations of the two afore-described aspects of Christian Ethics [3].

2) In the realm of Justice, the offering of Justice in material goods is relatively much easier a task than the task of offering Justice when it comes to psychosomatic human states. And it is precisely here

that creative ethos comes to facilitate the intellect and the spirituality of the administrator of the Justice under the concepts that have been described above {B-1}.

C. Practical Issues Associated with Justice

1) A **surplus** of well-qualified Legal Functionaries along with a surplus of resources is required so that Functionaries will be able to ponder on Justice **efficiently** and in a **sophisticatedly**. For, **the quality of Justice takes priority over the 'quantity'** of relevant court decisions in a restricted time-span. It is obvious, however, that the issuing of a court decision within a short amount of time significantly ameliorates the overall quality of Justice.

2) Legal functionaries and legal clerks should be given the appropriate incentives/motivation and also the appropriate motivation rewards, coupled with surplus resources. This is a **pivotal factor** for thoughtful and rightful allocation of Justice.

3) It is the **Essence** (Substantive + Procedural law) which strengthens the quality of Justice, and not the trivial or 'devious' details that breed unfairness instead.

BIBLIOGRAPHY

[1] "A contribution of theories of information and mathematical logic to the improvement of offering Justice" by Joseph-Christos Kondylakis & Georgia Sakarellou, in the proceedings of B conference of Greek Administrative Judges, on 2-December-1990, from page 162 .

[2] "The ancient Greek Philosophy", volumes A–B, by A. D. Krikoni, published by Kyromanos,Thessaloniki,Greece,2002

[3] "Themes of Christian Morality" by G. Mantiridis, B. G oultsis, S. Petrou, N. Tzoumakas, (for the last class of secondary education in Greece), published by the Greek Ministry of Education (Organization for publishing Educational Books),1991 .

ANNEX I

A letter of this author sent to the Pettitions' Committee of the European Parliament & to Others...

A SUMMARY OF MY PETITION TO THE EUROPEAN PARLIAMENT ENTITLED "VERY BIG BARRIERS PUT TO THE FUNDAMENTAL THEORETICAL SCIENTIFIC RESEARCH IN ONCOLOGY, E.T.C." SUBMITTED ON 22 MAY 2019

By Joseph-Christos Kondylakis, Research Scientist in Fundamental Scientific Research, B.Sc in Physics with Excellent degree from Aristotle University of Thessaloniki, Greece, M.Sc from McGill University of Canada financed with Canadian Scholarship, Succeeded with the 1st category of European Commission Competition COM/A/301 [...] Saturday-1-June-2019

My "Unified Theory of Oncology" was first created in 1983 and its main idea is that it considers the basic characterestic of Cancer illness, the abnormal greater multiplication rate of a certain group of cells, as malfunctioning(s) of the cell(s) molecular and sub-molecular informatics network(s) system...

My "Unified Theory of Oncology" and his creator(me) is confronding since 1983 Very Big Barriers in its/his development, its/his research, its/his promotion, in its/his resources and in his life. Very possibly most of to its/his imposed Very Big Barriers are with very bad intention(s) and many of them are described in the communications of this author with the Royal Netherlands Embassy in Greece, in the three criminal prosecutions in Athens, Greece & elsewhere and in his book of this author "War for the Destruction of (cognitive)

Intelligence" to be published about June 2019. In spite of the Very Big Barriers put to the Fundamental Theoretical Scientific Research in Oncology and to me, my "Unified Theory of Oncology" received very good letters of its appreciation from a "Giant' scientist in the medical informatics, the Professor Shigekoto Kaihara of University of Tokyo, Japan 1983, and a very good University Professor R.K. Mishra, of ALL-India Institute of medical Sciences, from India, 1984. It was presented in the European Scientific Symposium "Recent Advances in Diagnostic Imaging And Supportive Care in Oncology" 17-20 July 1997, Thessaloniki, Makedonia, Greece, it was published in the official scientific journal "Iatriko Bima", issue 84, of the Hellenic All Medical Doctors Association, about 2003 and in about 2015 the international applied scientific research in Oncology proved fully correct its original principles and considerations...

None mass media communications in Greece and Internationally want to publish my scientific research in oncology, possibly because of strong control of mass media communications from an international "elite" group with its own interests(refer to my relevant communications to the Royal Netherlands Embassy in Greece & elsewhere) ...

For comparison with my above mentioned oncology theory in 1983, the most widely fully advertised worldwide in the mass media communications, oncology research in 1983 was that of the University of Harvard in U.S.A. of its Prof. Christos Antoniades' research result that the...only cause of Cancer disease was the Harvard' "great" discovery of a..."pirate virus" ...which, of course, was proved to be a very silly idea...

Because the Fundamental Theoretical Scientific Research in Oncology is VITAL for the Humanity, because it provides a "compass" to significally orientate and accelarate the applied Oncology research toward to the its target of a possible cure of Cancer disease...

Because as McGill University of Canada announced to us about half of Canadians will be diagnosed with Cancer disease in the future...

Because it is Vital the theme that Very High Barriers are put in the

Fundamental Theoretical Scientific Research in Oncology to this author and to others...

Because I submitted on Wednesday-22-May-2019 my relevant Petition to European Parliament entitled "Very Big Barriers put to the Fundamental Theoretical Scientific Research in Oncology, E.T.C.".

Therefore for these reasons

Please assist us in:

[1] My above mentioned Petition to be Registered !

[2] My above mentioned Petition to be Accepted by the Members of European Parliament.

[3] Full Investigation to be initiated for the Very High Barriers put in the Fundamental Theoretical Scientific Research in Oncology and to this author...

[4] My Fundamental Theoretical Scientific Research entitled "Unified Theory of Oncology" to be widely promoted and further developed in European and World wide considerations...

Note: This author is available for any relevant additional information...

With Kind Regards

Joseph-Christos Kondylakis

ANNEX II

A letter sent of this author to the Petitions'Committee of European Parliament & to Others...

A SUMMARY OF MY PETITION TO THE EUROPEAN PARLIAMENT ENTITLED "WAR FOR THE DESTRUCTION OF (Cognitive) INTELLIGENCE, SUBMITTED ON 7 JUNE 2019

By Joseph-Christos Kondylakis, Nuclear Physicist & former Manager of Systems Design & Development in Canada ...] Friday-7-July-2019

ALL Human purposive Decisions are depended only on two factors : [1] The available information to the Human, and [2] The cognitive Intelligence of the Human.

The above statement is of paramound value, because any purposive human action is depended on human decision(s)...For instance the quality of life, the wars, the sciences & technologies and their development, the health, the economy, the environment, basically "everything"...

If someone(s) control the information to a human(s) [f.e. by controlling the mass media communications, including Internet tools) and simultaneously with War of Destruction of (cognitive) Intelligence transform a human(s) to almost Idiot, then Fully control as a Slave this human(s), organization(s), nation(s), E.T.C.

In a short phrase : Any purposive Development or Destruction is depended on human Decisions... therefore so is depended the Future of European Union, Humanity and planet Earth...

The main text of this petition is the original, very Critical book (in an attached file in this Petition) entitled "War for the Destruction of Intelligence" by Joseph-Christos Kondylakis, to be published about June 2019, which has arised from relevant scientific research and experiences of his author...

Because of the above reasons, we ask your help in:

[1] My this Petition to the European Parliament to be Registered.

[2] My this Petition to be Accepted by the Members of the European Parliament.

[3] Full wide & deep Investigations to be activated in All Themes of my this Petition and in the Themes of my book "War for the Destruction of Intelligence"(and in its references and references of references and so on) and in the life of this author as a clear example of an indicative victim of the "War for the Destruction of Intelligence"...

[4] European & Nations Defence to be established against the "War for the destruction of Intelligence", as this is related directly to the European & National Security...

[5] Further research & Investigations(past, present, future) to be done in the themes of "War for the Destruction of Intelligence" and its related Themes and its Consequences and also in Preventive considerations...

Note: This author is available for any relevant additional information...

With Kind Regards

Joseph-Christos Kondylakis